animal inn

THE
STORIES
OF A
TRAILSIDE
MUSEUM

animal inn

by
VIRGINIA
MOE

pictures by MILO WINTER

1946
BOSTON
HOUGHTON MIFFLIN COMPANY
The Riverside Press Cambridge

PRINTED IN THE UNITED STATES OF AMERICA

CAMBRIDGE · THE RIVERSIDE PRESS · MASSACHUSETTS

In the background of these stories are the boys and girls and other well-wishers of Trailside Museum. It is they who have brought to Trailside its richest treasures to be shared with all. Without them there could be no buckets of bullheads, baby birds, squirrelets, nests of cottontails, greenies, toad eggs, and all of the other orphaned and injured creatures of the wild who have found shelter in our living museum. It is they who have made each day exciting with new discoveries. They have hunted for and found the katydids, the meadow mice, the just-right crooked branch for the screech owls. They have cleaned cages, held medicine droppers and feeding forceps and broken legs, and watched and aided in the mysteries of birth and death. The small pensioners of Trailside that come to us, fearful and sometimes ferocious, are sure at last of the friendliness of these myriads of boys and girls who cannot talk their language, but who can play their kind of play.

And to the 'Huckleberry Pan' of them all this book is especially dedicated.

TO LITTLEJOHN

a good companion

to hold an injured blue jay while a splint is being placed on its broken leg. If you look as if you want to know about these things, you may be invited to feed a squirrel baby or one of a dozen hungry baby birds who haven't even grown their feathers yet. In every room you will be able to make friends with the birds and animals who make their homes in the Forest Preserve District of Cook County, Illinois. You will see them playing, eating, sleeping, caring for their young, and chattering among themselves.

For that is why the museum is here in Thatcher Woods — so that the boys and girls can find out about some of the interesting birds and animals, water creatures and insects, trees and plants, that you see when you leave the city to spend a day in the Forest Preserve. The city of Chicago and its suburbs have built westward from the shore of Lake Michigan for ten solid miles, but the city stops suddenly at Thatcher Avenue and there at the edge of Thatcher Woods is Trailside Museum, standing among the tall oaks and elms. Down in back of the museum is the pond and farther on through the woods is the Des Plaines River.

Thatcher Woods is only a small part of the thirty-five thousand acres of the Forest Preserve District. But even here, where the woods is now just a narrow green ribbon running through the city it has always been woodland. Now because it is a Forest Preserve it will always be undisturbed. Here the wild creatures have continued to make their homes in its hollow trees, under their roots and among their branches, and in dens along the river banks and in the river itself. Of all of these creatures most of us catch only a fleeting glimpse of some brown furry fellow scurrying into his hide-out or find only the footprints of those who prowl by night. But Trailside Museum, standing at the edge of this woods with all of its secrets, is there to discover a few of them.

The first Trailside Museum, although it was not so-called, was originated by Ansel Hall, a park naturalist, in Yosemite in 1921. This forerunner of a new idea was swiftly followed by others throughout the National Parks. In 1923 the Association of Museums became interested and began their program of outdoor education under the leadership of Hermon Carey Bumpus, who became the father of Trailside Museums in National Parks. It was Bumpus who coined the name Trailside Museum. Through his efforts in 1927, the famous Trailside Museum at Bear Mountain in the Palisades Interstate Park was established. William Carr, director of the museum since its beginning, has set many important keynotes for Trailsides later established by county, city, and state parks. Captain Charles G. Sauers, one of the country's leading conservationists and General Superintendent of the Forest Preserves since 1929, founded this Trailside Museum in Thatcher Woods in 1932, the first of its kind in the Midwest.

There are lots of interesting places where you may go to look and learn, but there are few places where you can have a lot of fun at the same time. Trailside is one, for it is almost entirely run by children. This is how it is done. Every day the museum blackboard reads something like this:

WORK FOR JUNIOR ASSISTANTS TODAY

Find a small hollow stump for the chipmunk
Repair the broken door on the owl cage and be careful not to startle them
Find a garden spider and look for the label in the files
Bathe the new robin's eyes with warm boric-acid solution
Gather dandelion and clover for wild cottontails
Shell field corn; be careful not to blister your hands
Handle the new skunk so that he will get tamer
Find woodchuck in basement cupboards, missing since yesterday
Get fresh sand and bedding for the mouse tank
Gather dry oak leaves for red squirrel's cage
Feed box turtles — see which they prefer; ground meat, grated carrot, apples
Collect twisted roots for meadow mice cage
Take fish that were trapped when river went down back to water

An Introduction to Trailside

These are just a few of the special chores for junior assistants, because every day most of the cages must have fresh sawdust or new bedding and often a washing with soap and water. Every day all of the outside cages must be raked and hosed. Then there is all of the food to prepare.

In the animal yard outside there are several cages, and one very large one is called the Play Cage. Nobody lives here, but on sunny days the junior assistants fill their shirts and pockets with guinea pigs and rabbits and turtles and young birds and take them outside to the Play Cage for exercise and sunshine. The junior assistants go inside, too, because this cage is for both animals and children.

At any time, especially during spring and summer, there may be new arrivals. To receive a box and to be the very first to open it and look in is always an exciting experience. Imagine seeing a baby weasel or a sassy young skunk for the first time! Someone has to find the right cage, the right kind of nest box, and all of the other things, such as branches and leaves or sand or sawdust, that we call 'cage furnishings.' All this means work for several junior assistants who try very hard to make the new guest feel at home in the kind of surroundings that best reproduce his original way of living.

Trailside never buys or collects its live exhibits. They are all brought to us or left on the doorstep in boxes after the museum closes or early in the morning before it opens. Many of the birds or animals have been injured and are picked up by the children who find them dragging a wing or hobbling about. Many of these die after a few days. But even some cases which seem hopeless do recover and can be released while others stay on as permanent guests at this Animal Inn. In our large hospital cage we keep those birds who would not be able to return to the wild because they are crippled. Here they live for many years on peaceful terms with a sparrow hawk that has been queen of the cage for six years. Scores of baby birds that are rescued when they fall from the nests are raised and released. These and the baby animals are the most fun and from them you can learn the things that are not found in any books, including this one. No book can tell you everything about any bird or animal. There are things you must see with your own eyes, feel with your own hands, and discover for yourself — and perhaps, I should add, feel in your own heart. The best part of learning in this way is that you begin to find out that things like snakes and mice, rats, toads, spiders, and slippery salamanders that you might have thought were better left alone are as interesting and likable as bluebirds, butterflies, and bunnies. It is not easy to dislike something that you feed and take care of and know all about!

Those who visit Trailside very often cannot help making friends with animals and birds because almost all of our pets are friendly. Those which are too old to get over their natural mistrust of people are only unhappy in captivity and so their stay with us is short. There are some birds and animals that long for freedom as soon as they grow up, even though they have never known the wild. These, too, are released. But there are those who seem to think that 'people are nicer than anybody,' and these are the permanent guests of Animal Inn.

Sometimes the woods and fields seem like a great stage-setting, a background for a pageant of the hundreds of little dramas that one knows are happening all around, but which require such sharp eyes and ears and so much patience to find. Most of us have to be content to learn by heart that background with its night and day scenes and its four great acts — which are the four seasons — and then piece the stories together one by one, getting acquainted with a few characters at a time wherever we chance to meet them.

If you are lucky enough to be able to have a wild pet or two, you can find out a great deal more about the part each plays in Nature's pageant. Wise and kind handling will make your pet affectionate and trusting. Food and surroundings that are as natural and comfortable as possible will keep him healthy and happy. When you have given him these things, then you will begin to have a little idea of how he acts in the wild. Your meadow mouse will make a nest of wool or paper, but he'll make you his own kind of nest if you give him dry grasses. It is more practical to keep ground squirrels in a cage with sawdust on a metal floor, but just give them a large aquarium half filled with soil and watch how the young ones who have never seen the earth will form a digging team for the construction of a tunnel that runs alongside the glass so that you can see the whole process. This will last but a day or two, for after much digging and refilling they will make all of their burrows away from the glass where you can't see how it is done.

If there is no end to your curiosity, there is never an end to the things your pets will teach you. But as you look through the cage wire, you must try also to see with one part of your mind how this or that action of your pet would fit into the wild background from which you have taken him. When he does strange and restless things and chews the woodwork, try to discover what he is seeking and what he would chew if he were in his own wild background. When he is gay and happy, you must, if he is a squirrel for instance, try to play with him in his own way and give him leaves to tumble in. Remember that you must make up to him in all sorts of ways for separating him from his own kind and for bringing him into a different world. You must give him new pleasures and contentments for those he has had to give up.

Even when one loves birds and animals, it is not easy to know or to find out how to care for them so that both of you will have fun being friends. I hope these true stories about a Trailside Museum will help you to discover more about wild creatures and their way of life.

CONTENTS

animal inn

1. John Rabbit

OF ALL THE ANIMALS who have lived and been loved at Trailside, there is no one animal that has drawn so much admiration and devotion as John, our white rabbit. He is really a part of the six-year-old institution started by John, the First, who died at the age of four years. John, the Second, has been heir to the name for four years, as it would not be Trailside without a John Rabbit. When I invited a little boy to give our first white rabbit a name, he decided that it should be called after his best friend, John. To call a rabbit John was a sort of shock to my sense of fitness concerning animal names, but there was no backing down on **an** invitation — so John it was from that day and John it will al-

1

ways be as long as there is a white rabbit to greet visitors at the door at Trailside. John knows his name and comes when he is called.

Our John has a large floor-cage with a metal tray bottom. The door of his cage is always open and the sign on it reads:

THIS IS JOHN'S HOUSE. IF HE IS NOT AT HOME LOOK FOR HIM IN THE BACK ROOM.

He often naps in his cage and he comes to it for his water, crushed oats, and vegetables, but the rest of the time he is not at home. White rabbits, when they have the freedom of the floor to roam at will, are very pleasant creatures to have about. Many of them establish definite sanitary habits if trained when very young and provided with a pan of clean sawdust or paper.

Like almost all white rabbits, John never does anything very exciting or unusual, but he has an air about him of never doing anything by chance. If you find him sitting in one of his favorite spots, you feel that this is the time of day he has set aside for sitting in this particular place. If you see him rounding the corner of the desk on his way somewhere, you are convinced that he knows exactly where he is going. Being a rabbit, simple as it is, seems to be a very serious business with John and it takes up all of his time!

Perhaps it is because everyone has wanted a rabbit at some time or other that John is such a favorite. Maybe it is because he has gentle, quiet ways. Sometimes I am sure it is his snowy whiteness that endears him to the public. Oddly enough, it is the grimiest of little boys with hands almost as black and sticky as a raccoon's paws who find John so irresistible. One little Italian boy told me that if John were his rabbit, he should be called 'Beautiful Angel.' By the evening of a warm summer's day, John's white coat begins to look somewhat shopworn, but before morning he has combed and licked it white again. Many persons, who do not know that a healthy animal never allows his coat to remain soiled, think that only a soap-and-water bath could keep him so clean.

At night, when John is no longer a Public Rabbit and can be

just a Private Rabbit, he takes care of this matter of a grubby coat. I have never seen him do it. But during the day I have often watched him clean his ears ... those long, delicate, pink-veined ears that point to the sounds they hear. How can anyone be so thoughtless as to pick up a rabbit by his ears simply because they are long and handy? It is not only probably very painful to the ears, but also injurious. Many long-eared rabbits have never been able to raise their ears after being mishandled in this way. The proper way to lift a rabbit is firmly to grasp the loose skin over the shoulder blades with one hand, to support the hind feet on the palm of the other hand. Even the biggest and toughest rabbits will think much more of you when you handle them in this way.

When John cleans his ears, he sits up on his hind legs and drops one ear straight down, exactly as if he were pulling a string that was tied to it. Then he grasps his ear between those two stiff-looking front paws and, bending it under his chin, he manages to clean it inside and out with his tongue and moistened paws. At first glance you can't imagine how paws with such dirty fur on the undersides (for rabbits show no bare toes) could aid in the washing. If you watch carefully, you can see that the washing is done as a cat does it — with the clean, inner side of the paws that never touches the floor.

When John was little and limber and floppy, he would lie on his back on your knees, while you gently twisted his long legs up about his ears into pretzel shapes. Totally relaxed, he would let himself be carried like a dead rabbit, flat on his back with his head hanging loosely. He is much too large and plump now for the pretzel bending, but John still plays dead and loves it. Another dreadful thing he seems to enjoy is to be carried about like a doll, wearing a blond wig tied on with a handkerchief. Every so often the boys dress him up and sit holding him, fascinated by that clown-white face, with half-closed pink eyes and the colored wig which makes him resemble nothing human nor animal. You must not think that because of this John is a nambypamby. He has very decided ideas about having his own way and resents with loud growls a

3

broom that routs him from his corner. He will even strike out with his sharp-clawed front feet and growl when his food dishes are touched while he is eating.

The rest of John's life is very dignified and orderly and consists of being petted and stroked by children who bring him sacks of lettuce and carrots. Somehow no one ever talks nonsense with John. But his friends, who have learned just how to hold and balance him and keep him forgetful of his unrabbitlike position as they grasp him, are learning that strange magic which comes into the hands of those who are growing familiar with animals. It is the magic of awareness and perception, of strength and gentleness.

One of the most important things in John's life are his 'chewing sticks.' These are sturdy twigs and branches cut fresh once a week and placed on the floor where he can nibble away at the bark until they are bone-white. The teeth of rabbits and their close relatives, rodents, continue to grow all of their lives because, in the gnawing of hard grains, nuts, and bark, their teeth are constantly being worn down and must be replaced. Pet squirrels, rats, rabbits, and all the rest of this great chisel-tooth tribe, if fed only soft food, will gnaw wood or even metal in an effort to keep their teeth from growing too long. A careful check is kept of John's teeth in order to make sure that they are short, sharp, and of even length, because, if he were to break off one of his four long incisor teeth, their growth would be uneven and the teeth would be thrown out of line. This happened to the first John. Before the broken tooth was discovered, the other three were permanently crooked. Each week it was necessary to clip the teeth. After a year, they became so curled and distorted from lack of proper use that one pierced his lip and the infection caused his death.

An important part of John's daily life is his full water dish. A rabbit needs in proportion to his size five times as much water as a human being, and yet many rabbits must depend upon the water in green vegetables because their owners believe that water is bad for them. How should you like always being more or less thirsty? All captive animals, even those of the desert — who never drink because there is no water and depend upon dew and succulent plants along with a special body chemistry that turns the starches to water in their bodies — should always have water within reach. The dry air of heated rooms, the never entirely natural food of the pet wild animal, often cause unnatural cravings for water. Some of our squirrels whose cages are in the coolest locations rarely touch their water, while those near a hot-air register become frantic when their water bottles go dry. A prairie dog we once had never so much as sniffed at his water dish for months. I was almost convinced that supplying him with water was a waste of effort on my part and an inconvenience to him, because all he ever did was to step in it and look disgusted. Then one day he changed his mind and developed a thirst which he satisfied by one long deep drink every day for the rest of his life.

Friendliness between rabbits and cats or dogs is a very common occurrence. The first John dearly loved dogs and would risk his life to win their friendship. He would follow my dog, Wendy, at top speed from room to room until he fell exhausted, but the dog ignored him with supreme disdain. Occasionally a gentle dog whose owner could vouch for his good behavior was allowed into the museum, and the first John liked nothing better than having his face and ears licked by the dog if he happened to be one of those dogs with an affectionate tongue. The first John also liked Vickie, the cat, and although he took many beatings from her claws and teeth, he was always content to nap close against her on the hot-air register after the fun was over. There are many cases of pet rabbits, both wild and domestic, keeping the upper hand over the household cats and dogs who turn tail and yelp when attacked by the mulish kicks that a rabbit can deliver with his hind legs.

John the Second hobnobs with the skunks and was a great chum of Bambi, the fawn, during the several months he was with us. At night they wandered through the dark rooms of the museum, always within a few feet of each other. When Bambi stopped, John waited. When Bambi lay down, John hopped around him in circles, and then lay down to wait until his friend was ready to stroll on.

A squirrel will play back and never ceases to invent new tricks. A coon has a face of many expressions and the manners of a clown. A guinea pig sings like a cage of canaries and has the most laughable of animal faces. But a white rabbit with pink eyes is the animal everyone loves and calls by name and comes back to see over and over again. I wonder, if next to those famous immortal ones — Peter Rabbit, Thumper, and the white rabbit in *Alice in Wonderland* — our John hasn't more friends than any other rabbit in the world!

2.

Chuckles,

The Woodchuck

CHUCKLES, THE WOODCHUCK, when he was very young, was the fat boy of the Trailside family. From his own standpoint he had a very interesting babyhood, for although he was only half-tame, for some months he was an outstanding character in his curious blend of native wildness and at times aggressive sociability.

Nobody interfered with him. Nobody tried very hard to make a pet of him, and everybody was immensely flattered when he chose to make a pet of them, because Chuckles was very choosy about his friends and, indeed, about everything that he did. Like some humans he had a house that he never lived in. It was a very comfortable cage with a strawlined sleeping-box up off the floor and a sliding metal tray floor filled with sawdust. Although the cage door was always open so that he could walk in and out whenever he wanted to, he didn't even visit it very often. When he did, no one ever shut the door because he immediately set to work to open it, and after Chuckles is through working there isn't much left but a hole and a little pile of shavings and chips. This is hard on most things, but it keeps his long teeth sharp and short, for he is another member of the great Chisel-Tooth tribe, the rodents.

Chuckles also used his teeth to persuade people to do things or not to do things. A sly nip on fingers or ankles and we all ceased to argue. Chuckles always won. But we didn't mind, because we understood that this was what his mother had taught him and it would always be his way. His stay with her in the meadow den had lasted until he was old enough to eat clover and alfalfa and other green foods and no longer needed her to nurse him, but in that time she taught him many things that no one could ever have untaught. As a baby, when he was playful and even a bit affectionate, he was always rough and often pinched too hard with his sharp white teeth. But always at the back of his mind was, and still is, the idea of defense.

Chuckles is built for defense. He has no neck to speak of and each cheek is as broad as his face. Like a coon's, all of the skin of his body is very loose. When you want to carry him in a hurry, you just pick him up by the skin of his back and carry him like a satchel. That is about the only way that you can carry him when he doesn't want to be picked up, because, unless you have a firm hold on this loose skin, it is very easy for him to turn around in it and nip you.

His rolling walk and short legs make him look like a woolly bear caterpillar, but in spite of his fat, soft, shapeless appearance, he and his kind have the speed, limberness, and strength of a wrestler. Any dog that has attacked a wild chuck has found this out. It is said that matched in weight no single dog can down him. Even several powerful dogs will suffer the punishment of slashing teeth before the chuck goes down in defeat under their combined attack. Brave as all animals are when cornered, the chuck is rather fearless under any circumstances. If a farmer's truck garden suits his purpose, there he will dig his den. There he will live for years under the very eyes of the dogs and the farmer's sturdy sons, rarely going as far as fifty yards from his burrow entrance, for chucks are the greatest of all stay-at-homes just as they are the greatest of den-diggers. Any dweller of dens in the wild is grateful for an abandoned woodchuck's den.

One may imagine how infuriating it must be to a farm dog to have to share the premises with a garden woodchuck such as Chuckles. In keeping with the woodchuck character, he never trots about aimlessly. His walk is always slow, stolid, even pompous. Each foot is planted down with a deliberate lack of stealth, although he often pauses in the middle of a step and with raised head sniffs and listens. There is no peering about or turning the head. Only a sudden or unfamiliar sound or sight destroys his dignity. At top speed he skids noisily to cover. You have a feeling that he is chuckling to himself while he runs, because there is something gay and elated about his pell-mell retreat. Sometimes he prefers to stand his ground and challenge trouble. His tail begins to stiffen out and waggle. Then it stands straight up with all of the hairs bristling like a bottle brush that means 'Beware.' His relaxed body undergoes a swift change as his jowls and shoulders seem to grow larger than his hind quarters. And when he charges and gallops off, he has a curious resemblance to a miniature buffalo. I have both seen and done some wild and high-stepping dances when Chuckles was in a charging mood.

Like many animals Chuckles has his own distinctive smell noticeable even to our dulled human senses. Sometimes on long, rainy days, the junior assistants play a game of smells. A boy is blindfolded and tries to identify each animal by smell alone. Chuckles smells like tomato soup! — but you must bury your nose in the fur about his neck to catch it.

When he was little, Chuckles spent some time every day taking care of his toenails. In the privacy behind my desk where all of our pets go to be alone, he would lie on his back and nibble his nails down to the length that pleased him. But so far as I know, his grooming stops there. Nobody has ever seen Chuckles washing himself as do the rabbits and squirrels. After eating, he sometimes licks his fingers, but that is usually because they have something good-tasting on them. His skin is usually clean and white. Every few weeks Chuckles has a bad case of dandruff. All of his skin lifts up in flakes and drops off. Then he likes very much to be scratched or combed, and when all of the dry, dead skin has peeled away his skin is as sleek and clean as if it had been scrubbed. If this is what happens to wild woodchucks, then it must be very convenient for them living as they do in contact with the earth in burrows deep in the ground. It may be, of course, that in their natural environment the oils from the skin take care of any dirt that might coat it. The fur on a woodchuck's underarms and belly, especially in summer, is much thinner than that on the back, and no doubt this also makes for a cleaner hide.

When Chuckles first came to the museum, he was a lonely, sad baby, who had been snatched from the entrance to his mother's den and sold to a pet shop. In the cage next to him was our motherless raccoon baby who was no happier. Both had been here a few days when I put them in the soft, bouncy nest of a little old, fat prairie dog who had always lived alone. Her name was Muffins, but for obvious reasons she was nicknamed Muffie Puffie. Muffie accepted her strangely assorted family with the same sweet temper in which she accepted everything. The babies rolled with delight and contentment in this more homelike way of living. All animal babies want to live in a heap. They feel warmer and safer in a heap, and then there is always the fun of waking up out of a sound sleep and chewing someone's ear or having a rough-and-tumble wrestling match. When a hot spell came along, they slept all day in a row on their backs like three little poisoned pigs. The woodchuck and the raccoon spent a short and happy babyhood in the grassy nest of the prairie dog. But soon they outstripped her in size and their games became too rough even for the woodchuck. So the two were separated.

Chuckles then began his life alone and probably gave not a thought to his former bedfellows. Woodchucks are solitary animals who do not care much for the company of even their own families. In the wild the father chuck has his own den all to him-

10

self and baby woodchucks leave the mother's den at a tender age to make their own way in the world.

After a few weeks in the new cage, Chuckles in his daily wanderings found a much better spot in the basement. This was a dark corner far back under a filing-case in a large closet. The warped spring door in the closet suited him fine. He could open it with his long claws and when it closed behind him there was no danger of nosy, sniffing skunks or curious squirrels or any other animal bothering him. With a few stolen dustcloths, papers, and a feather pillow which he opened and emptied, Chuckles made himself a snug nest and spent much time there, growing in the night as the corn grows.

His appetite at this time was unbelievable. At a half-hour sitting he would begin with a large bowl of bread and milk and continue on without a pause through two bananas, two carrots, and two apples. The slow but steady change of contour as he grew

11

broader in girth during his meal was very
noticeable. As he started on the first
banana, he sat with head up and spine as
straight as a ramrod, holding his food
squirrel-fashion in his two black and
almost hairless hands. By the time he
got to the last slice of apple, he had
become a study in curves and often
finished by sitting so far back on his
spine that his hind feet no longer
reached the floor, but lay with soles
turned up. At the end
of the meal he would
waddle away and prop
himself up in a corner
to lick his fingers. But
sleep and contentment would swiftly
overcome him, and like a sack of grain
that has not been set firmly on its base, he would slowly sag into
a position in which he neither sat nor lay down, but was just 'all of
a heap.'

Oddly enough, neither Chuckles nor any other woodchuck I
have known was ever greedy or possessive about food. Even the
tamest squirrels are fearful of being robbed and will chatter and
scratch at your hands, but a woodchuck may be freely petted
while eating. Take his carrot from his hands and he will simply
pick up another one. He will, if you wish, take a companionable
grip on your finger with one of his hands, if you will help him to
hold his carrot with your other hand. I was once on more than
speaking acquaintance with an old grizzled chuck who, in spite of
the violent protests of the dog, came to live under the summer cot-
tage where I was staying. At four o'clock in response to my whistle, he would come out to feed from my hand. Like Chuckles he
was perfectly willing to hold hands while he ate. This tolerance
while eating may be due to the woodchuck's natural life in the midst

of plenty. Food is always at his doorstep. He need not hunt nor fight for it and he never wants more than he can eat on the spot because he lays up no winter store. Famine holds no fears for him. When winter fields lie bare and frozen, he is in the deep sleep of hibernation down under the sleeping roots of clover.

As a result of this healthy appetite, Chuckles's baby coat was quickly replaced. His new brown winter coat glittered with long silvery guard hairs and underneath the silky surface fur was a soft fluffy undercoat. The coppery fur about his chest and forearms shone with metallic brightness. Short fur covered the inner sides of his legs and broad belly, and when he sat up, the direction of its growth showed like a zipper line down the whole length of his body. Yet even in winter the woodchuck's fur hasn't the denseness of growth found in the coats of other animals. The hairs are widely spaced and skin can always be seen when the hairs are parted. Although the tough hide was used in pioneer days for whip handles and mitten backs, the pelt is of use to no one except the woodchuck — which is just as well, because for him it is a glorious cloak of fur. In it he appears to be what you might consider a very prosperous animal, the luxuriant fur on his jowls giving him an air of being buried in a high-collared and very expensive fur coat. But like many expensive things it doesn't wear well and by spring he looks like a shabby motheaten buffalo.

One day Chuckles made his first and only whistle when he was dragged upstairs and placed in his cage against his will. The whistle of a woodchuck is a shrill one exactly the way most boys can whistle, except that at the end of it he vibrates all over and rattles inside and sometimes chatters his teeth together. We once had a woodchuck who used to whistle sharply at three o'clock for service if her food was late in arriving. The whistle is generally considered to indicate warning or threat and is one of those calls in nature that is not commonly heard.

It wasn't long before two skunks, also on the prowl for winter quarters, learned to open Chuckles's closet door which had warped open a bit farther. So when they moved in, Chuckles moved out.

13

A hermit by nature, he could bear no company even when asleep. For a long time he searched every corner of the big house where the Trailside animals live, and after two days, when he couldn't be located, we knew that he had found the new den. On the third day he appeared and vanished again. This went on for some time. We would call and open doors and cupboards and turn over boxes, and suddenly there would be Chuckles standing in the middle of the floor looking sleepy. After a few times of seeing Chuckles really walk out of an empty cupboard into which we had just looked, we crawled in and found that he had discovered a hidden opening in the built-in cupboard that went back in between the basement foundation wall and the wainscoting. Here was the hide-out. One night the cupboard door was shut too tightly. Chuckles made a neat little arched opening where the two doors joined. At night he emptied wastebaskets and sometimes took pictures from the bulletin board. Once he made off with some un-opened mail and we haven't yet found out whose letters they were.

All through the autumn Chuckles was torn between two ideas. He wanted solitude, quiet, and darkness, but he also wanted to be up and about to eat. At noon as regular as clockwork he came up-stairs to the museum and climbed up in his favorite place by the window and spent half an hour gazing peacefully out at the land-scape. He had learned that at this hour the museum was closed and he could have it to himself. At five he would again appear. Baby-hood was falling from him more swiftly every day and he resented violently everyone but me. In an effort to overcome his un-sociableness, I began to carry him upstairs to my apartment in the evening.

He immediately found that the big, low couch was an excellent place to hide under. There he would lie facing the room and just under the front of the couch. After much coaxing he would begin to snort and puff and then out he would dash to nip a finger and back up to safety with about the same technique as a steam roller. It is amazing how fast he can throw himself into reverse. After only two evenings he began to see the possibilities of turning a living-room into a game-room. Animals quickly learn to associate certain signs and the human voice with pleasant things. A tap on the floor, the sound of his name — which he has always known — or the little movement I made with my hand, and out Chuckles would dash to roll and tumble and nip and tease, turning up his wide belly, always a sure sign of trust.

Stopped in a rush by my thrust-out hand, he would lightly summersault. But always after a roughhouse he would retreat to cover and rest flat and relaxed, chin on the floor, and a look of anticipation on his usually unexpressive face while he gained breath for the next attack. He never came out unless called. It seemed a part of the game to let me call and coax and then to rush out and surprise me. When he was tired of play, he would examine the whole room, indifferent to the dog stalking at his heels. Finally climbing up on the table, he would sit up beside a bowl of late autumn flowers and delicately draw down one or two blossoms to within reach of his mouth and eat them. He would then stretch out on a corner of the table or on the sill of the open window and stare straight ahead.

At this point most animals would enjoy being petted and stroked. Not Chuckles. Not any woodchuck I have ever known. Instead of falling into the usual trance produced in other animals by petting and scratching, the woodchuck seems annoyed and restless. The prairie dog — at least the older ones, who seem not to understand play with humans at all — are slaves for attention. They crave it, coax for it, and sit up and beg and bark for a hand pat and will lie indefinitely soaking up all the affection they can get. They love the company of other creatures. No animal that I know is so completely sociable and can radiate so much sheer pleasure in human companionship as a prairie dog, but in them I have found no sense of humor like a woodchuck's mischievous deviltry and gay make-believe. Love and hate or anger are real to the prairie dog. The woodchuck mixes his so that neither is quite real. His anger and enmity are amusing and his love is difficult and painful.

During a few days of the first cold weather, Chuckles denned up and failed even to come out for food. I grew tired of coaxing him every night, so there was some time during which he was not invited upstairs. Perhaps he sometimes waited at the door at the top of the stairs. I never thought to look. One evening the door happened to be open and in walked Chuckles. He then became a regular visitor promptly at eight o'clock.

His sanitary habits were beyond reproach. He soon found the cat's pan of sawdust and always made use of it when upstairs. One morning I wakened to find that Chuckles was just getting up too. Unknown to me he had spent the night in my room. He crawled out from under the dresser, yawned, and slowly walked down the long hall and through two rooms to the cat's pan which he made use of in his very fastidious manner. Another night he was accidentally locked in the living-room. His small, inoffensive droppings were discovered in a corner carefully covered with a square inch of frayed-out cotton insulation which he had evidently spent some time in removing for that purpose from a heavy light-cord.

It isn't every evening that one has time to entertain a woodchuck and so there were nights when the door was closed, but Chuckles had only one idea about doors. It was better to give in than to have Chuckles get out his burglar tools and chew it open. Some evenings he had no desire to play, but would just lie under the couch for an hour or two and appear to be listening to the radio. Sometimes he wasn't ready to leave when I dumped him outside the door and he would squeal with rage and manage to dart back in several times before I could shut it. I've had a fawn follow me upstairs and dart through the door and into the kitchen for his morning bottle of milk, but that never seemed as fantastic as the sound of a half-tame animal — and one of the few strictly daytime animals at that — scratching and thumping at the closed door simply because he wanted to join the family circle.

As winter really set in, Chuckles's evening visits grew rarer and finally ceased. But mornings when he came out to eat while I was preparing food for the other animals, he would sometimes pester me for attention by pulling at my ankle or dogging my footsteps. Perhaps he wanted a good thumping on the ribs, perhaps a very little bit of scratching. If he was in an especially fine humor, he would shut his eyes and gently nibble my hand or sleeve. Sometimes he wanted to play tag. I have never known an animal who was so fascinated by playing tag and so clever at it, although perhaps I should call it 'stomp the leader.' As fast as one could run within the confines of several rooms, Chuckles would follow churring queerly to himself with a sound like the throbbings under a streetcar just before it begins to move. It never seemed to occur to Chuckles to cut a corner short. He would run exactly in your footsteps, no matter how intricate the turns and twists, and stop dead in his tracks when you did. Chuckles might carry a chip on his shoulder and show very bad temper toward all animals and people, he might want to live his own life and be left alone, but every so often the fat little hermit got tired of his own company.

Winter wore on. Chuckles's desire for privacy caused him to prefer to eat when not even I was looking. Later his appetite grew sketchy and for several days at a time food was left untouched. He was trying very hard to answer the winter call of sleep that comes so strongly to the woodchucks wherever they may be. Of course, his response in denning up cannot compare with the true hibernation which is a state of deep sleep bordering on death itself. In hibernation the heart beats only four or five times a minute in contrast to the waking hours when there are eighty beats a minute. In hibernation breathing occurs about once in five minutes, whereas a woodchuck, when awake, breathes thirty to forty times a minute and even one hundred times when excited.

The first day of spring finds Chuckles much thinner than when his appetite was at its full peak. During the winter he has lost all of his long guard hairs. His coat has a worn, dull, woolly look. It has been weeks since we have had even a chat. The rare times when I have seen him out of his den seem to fill him with dismay and he scuttles back into retreat in lightning haste. Perhaps when summer comes he will remember our old friendship, but I think not. Many a woodchuck has been kept as a pet for years, but what in Chuckles's babyhood was overrough play is in his adulthood a real bar to any safe and pleasurable relationship.

When June fields and pastures are green and lush, Chuckles will find himself free among the rolling acres of a farm where there are several woodchuck dens at the top of a hill and the sun shines warm on the deep clover. He will be happy there only because what he learned of human ways and friendliness came just too late. In an animal's makeup the milk of the mother leaves little room for an understanding of the milk of human kindness. There is no compromise.

3.

The Opossum's Creed

IF YOU LOOK DEEPLY into the eyes of an opossum, there is a strange distant look that gives you the feeling that he is living in the past — that he doesn't belong here in this modern world. What an ancient creed opossums must have! Those eyes are different from the eyes of any of our other American animals. They are as shiny as shoebuttons — not like eyes with the light of intelligence behind them. They don't even change much after the animal is dead. The 'possum acts as if he, too, feels that he is in the wrong place. Whether he is young or old, tame or newly captured, he shrinks and winces and draws back at every friendly move in his direction. With wide-open mouth he stares and stares and never turns his back on you. At Trailside, we usually put a label on a

19

'possum cage which reads: 'This 'possum is acting perfectly natural, even though it looks blind and has its mouth open.'

Of course, the 'possum is really somewhat out of place now, but there was a time when he wasn't a freak in this world, for he and his kind were plentiful. Fifty million years ago 'possums weren't much different from what they are today. At that time all of the mammals or furry animals were marsupials, a word which means pouch-bearers.

Like 'possums these marsupials carried their young ones in a sort of pocket or pouch of skin that covered the belly of the mother animal. Then some great change in the earth's surface caused part of the land along the coast of Asia to break away and form what is now the island continent of Australia. After that these first pouched animals who had lived all over the world began to die out and their places were taken by the animals without pouches similar to those we know today. 'Possums in South America, Central America, and North America simply stayed on the earth and continued to carry their young ones in a pouch — which isn't difficult while they are young, because at birth they are no bigger than a honey bee and eighteen of them can be carried in a teaspoon! The 'possums also went on living in Australia with a whole set of strange creatures with strange names whose close relatives are alive today — such as the wombat, the koala, the bandicoot, the kangaroo, the wallaby, and the cuscus, all of which have pouches. The 'possum, then, is a sort of living fossil and a link with the faraway past.

And so, you see, his creed *is* an ancient one and a strange one. Every 'possum we have ever known at the museum acted exactly like every other 'possum we ever knew or heard about. They live their slow, secret lives; they think slowly and secretly, and they move in the same manner, always watching and waiting for you to go away before they do what they intended to do before you came along and looked at them. They seem to fit the weird, spooky music that usually announces a ghost story on the radio and to belong in a haunted house full of cobwebs and shadows.

One cold, winter day an injured 'possum was brought to the

museum. When it died, the body was placed in the ash can at the rear of the building. That day the ashes were removed, but later, when I went out to empty some papers, I found the dead 'possum still in the refuse can. I thought it was odd that the collectors had taken everything but the body. I reached in and picked it out by the tail. Of course, it was stiff. I turned it right side up and marveled that there could be so little change even in death. The four feet stuck out straight, the back curved to fit my hand, the dull eyes stared, and the pale mouth hung open. I was about to put it back in the can when something flashed me a warning that this was not a dead animal, but a *live* one 'playing 'possum.' When I took off my heavy glove, I found the body warm. The 'possum seemed to know that I knew, and although it never once relaxed its stiffness, its eyes moved ever so slightly. I placed it under a basket against the house, where I expected it to stay until it could make for freedom after dark. A few minutes later, when I looked out of the window, it was gone, although I suppose it was crouching close by in one of the leafless winter trees where its weathered gray coat camouflaged it perfectly.

The minute a 'possum knows he is being looked at, his mouth snaps open. You can't tell whether he is afraid or trying to scare you. It is a large mouth, very pale, and is filled with many small sharp teeth. They are very primitive teeth and he has more of them than any other animal. When little, a 'possum makes small, soft noises. As he grows larger, the sound grows louder and more unpleasant. Try moaning with your mouth open and you will have a good imitation.

His hand-washing is about the only interesting thing he does in captivity and is quite different from the swift way of squirrels and other rodents. The 'possum puts up a hand to each side of his cheek and draws it down along the sides of his tongue as he sticks it out. In and out goes the tongue, and up and down move his hands — he does not lick them as much as rub them on his wet tongue. Now and then he stops and licks between his fingers which are always pinky clean. Somehow, one never speaks of a 'possum's paws, they

21

are so much like hands. There are five, pink hairless fingers that spread as wide as a kewpie doll's. Short black fur covers the wrist and back of the hand, making it look as if he were wearing fingerless lace mitts such as ladies wore in the old days. His hind feet have five toes also, and they are more like hands than his front feet because the thumb spreads away from the fingers and has no claw like the rest of the fingers.

With such clever-looking fingers, you would expect him to sit up and eat like a squirrel, but he doesn't. He first picks up his food with his mouth, and then, if the chunk is too large, he grasps it with one hand and tugs while he pulls with his teeth He never uses his hands to carry food to his mouth. But his tail, much like a rat's and scaly and bare of fur except for a few sparse hairs that only show upon close examination, is the only American animal's tail that can hook over a branch and support its owner. A few people have seen a 'possum using its tail to drag a bundle of nesting material to the den. A mother 'possum is often seen carrying a litter of twelve young ones on her back, all hanging on with their tails to her tail which she arches over them.

When our twelve baby 'possums arrived, we didn't know how many we had because at first they were all in their mother's pouch and it was several days before they came out in the open. This mother was in a sad condition when she was brought to Trailside, for she had been kept in a small filthy cage. All we could see of the babies were a handful of the dirtiest of little tails dangling from her pouch. Everyone agreed that it would be a week before she could be brought up from the basement to the museum, but as it wasn't convenient to keep her in the basement, a large, clean cage floored with sawdust was arranged and she was left alone with plenty of food and water.

When I returned four hours later to look in on her, I found the most beautiful example of what it means to an animal to have a chance to live according to its creed. That creed, especially when there are young ones to care for, is cleanliness. Anyone seeing the 'possum for the first time that night would have thought that she had had weeks of the finest care in the cleanest surroundings. The five babies on her back were wet to the skin and every nose, tail, and toe was as pink as a rose. Out of her pouch dangled several tails like little pink fishing worms and she herself was scrubbed until she glowed. Although none of the food had been touched, the large dish of water was empty. How a mother animal must suffer if she is unable to keep herself and her babies clean when every instinct tells her how important it is!

In the short time that we had the mother 'possum at Trailside, I noticed a few very interesting things. One was that, as the babies climbed out of the pouch to nap on her back, they usually arranged themselves in such a way that there was never too much weight on either side. If there were eight on her back, four of them were on her right and four on her left side. If one dropped off and crawled back into the pouch for more milk, another would move over. No one ever saw her wash her babies, but I often found them still damp from their evening bath. In the morning, she was a very sound sleeper and until nine-thirty she would be lying flat on her back with the babies spread out over her open pouch, hanging on to the twelve long nipples inside of it. Never once was she seen to look at a baby, nuzzle it, or act in what from our human standpoint we would call a motherly way. When we had had her about a week, two very tiny 'possums, about two and a half inches long, were brought in. Their mother had been killed on a railroad track. The first night alone in their warm cage, they hissed constantly. It sounded exactly like an electric fly trap on a screen door. I never again heard this call, so it must have been brought on by their extreme hunger and dismay because they had lain for many hours beside the dead mother.

These still blind infants were placed in the cage of the mother 'possum. They were barely able to walk and stumbled about in all directions without seeming to sense that she was near. Blind baby rats, no bigger than a small thumb, have no difficulty crawling back into their own nest, but these babies had to trip over the mother's tail and follow it blindly until they found the heap of sleeping babies. They must have finally smelled the warm milk, for they dove into the heap and disappeared and were not heard from again for several days.

During all this time, the mother made no move and showed no sign of any feeling, not even the mildest curiosity. She must have seen them, as she had been looking in their direction when they were put in her cage. The next day, she seemed very weak, and when we watched we found that she had great difficulty in eating. As her own young ones were now sampling the fruit, bread, raw meat, fish, and cow's milk that was placed in the cage each night, we removed them to a separate cage. With her pouch empty, her extreme thinness showed very plainly, in spite of the heavy fluffy coat. During the last few days, as she grew steadily weaker, and as we kept her hot-water bottle warm, fed her what milk she could swallow from a doll's bottle, turned her from left to right to wash and comb her fur, we got to know the 'possum very well. She was a nice old thing, even though she looked like the wolf in grandmother's bedclothes as she lay wrapped in a blue blanket. We gave her one baby for company so that she wouldn't feel too lost without her large family. She was the only 'possum that ever showed any reaction to anything we ever tried to do. Because she couldn't clean herself and because the milk continued to flow, we had to bathe her pouch twice a day with warm water. As soon as we began, she would turn over on her back and in the way that animals have, she made us feel that she appreciated this which she could not do for herself. But she was the most difficult patient we ever had. There was never any change of expression on her face to tell us whether she was pleased or annoyed or unhappy. We were sorry when she died, partly because we had had so little time to learn her way of life, but mostly because every member of our Trailside family, down to the smallest mouse, is an important individual, and all the boys who share in their care feel the loss when there is an empty cage to be cleaned and put away in the basement.

At the time we separated the mother from her young, we placed the two foster babies in the nest cage of two baby gray squirrels.

THE OPOSSUM'S CREED

The almost hairless 'possums seemed to need the added warmth of the two larger squirrels. Cold and clammy to touch, with weak, sightless eyes, the hairless 'possums were anything but endearing creatures in those days. Their skin wasn't pinkish like most animal babies — it was a peculiar shade of yellow and peach color — and their bodies were hard as an unripe pear. They didn't even smell pleasantly! But all of these unattractive features seem to be the stuff which goes to make a fine 'possum, for at last they began to change, grew hair, and got soft podgy bellies. Their hard, thick little ears unfolded and looked like bits of black-and-white oiled paper.

Life became much simpler when the 'possums learned to drink alone. For weeks we had struggled with them and they had struggled back. Only a few drops at a time could we get into them and their manner of feeding was wonderful to watch. They would claw the air, grope, clench their little goblin fists, wring their hands, pull their noses, and drag at their lower jaws. Everything that could be done to prevent a successful feeding they did, and yet they never really resisted. They just didn't seem to understand. Baby squirrels and ground squirrels know exactly what to do. When shown a medicine dropper of milk for the first time, they stand up and take hold of it with both hands and empty it in a wink, but not 'possums. The funniest trick of all was the way the little male would get hold of both hind legs or his tail or all three and pull them up over his head while drinking from the dropper. Their alligator-like mouths so bristling with sharp teeth seemed to split from ear to ear and most of the milk ran out into their ears.

In raising young animals, we try to imitate as nearly as possible the way they would live if they were in their own nests. Warmth, darkness, cleanliness, and undisturbed sleep, except when they are taken up for feedings, are important. After days of this care, the 'possums began to grow more active. When the grays at the age of about ten weeks began to suck bread and milk from a dish and to gnaw on fruit, the much tinier 'possums also began to eat under their own power. Now that the dark nesting period was over, the four

were placed in a larger cage and the little squirrels grew very active
as they climbed and leaped about in kitten play. The 'possums
were often forced to join in the games. Indeed, they often *were*
the games. Squirrels are very deft with their hands, and occasionally the tiny 'possums were made to play the part of croquet
balls just as the hedgehogs in *Alice in Wonderland*. The 'possums
didn't ever learn how to play, but neither did they mind being
stepped on, tumbled about, and accidentally buried and dug up
as the squirrels busily covered and uncovered nuts in the old
sweater that was their bed. The 'possums went right on sleeping,
eating, or slowly washing themselves. At night they gathered
about them what few wits they had and crawled to the choice spot
at the bottom of the heap. The only thing they minded was being
crowded away from the food dish, and as baby squirrels are extremely greedy and almost never get their fill, but eat until their
bellies are shiny and tight, the much tinier 'possums had to work
their way to the food, even though it meant crawling between the
legs of the squirrels, who braced themselves shoulder to shoulder
and guzzled in a sort of blind frenzy. Slowly the 'possums would
lap up the milk, slowly they would waddle back to bed and clean
themselves up, curl up and go to sleep.

The other 'possum babies who were orphaned did everything
alike and at the same time. All day they slept in a large wooden
chopping-bowl piled up neatly like 'possum pie. If one slipped over-
board, he just hung there upside down, fast asleep, until he fell out
completely. About four o'clock they all got up and ate and washed
and then went back to bed. As soon as it grew dark, they all got
up again and began to walk their exercising wheel. I say walk,
because no 'possum would dream of running a wheel. With them,
the wheel-walking seemed to be a chore and they did it in a slow,
plodding, bored way. Some rode as the wheel went around. At
night when they were all startled by a sudden light, they all
looked in the same direction, all hissed open-mouthed, and all
cringed at the same instant. We never tired of watching them at
night, twelve little ghostly heads pale and pointed and trembling

slightly as they sniffed with black noses; twenty-four round black eyes with a point of light reflected in them; twenty-four ears like crinkly black petals tipped with white and every face bristling with silvery whiskers. Up to a certain age, 'possums have wistful elfish faces with a vague expression of wonderment which they seem to lose suddenly overnight and then become just plain homely and unlovely.

When little, they will cling to a boy's shoulder or a little girl's long curls and hang there for hours, seemingly very content. It is a pity that they haven't the brains to be better pets, as they are rather nice to hold with their warm, soft silvery fur and the sort of catlike feel of their bodies. But the opossum's creed, although he learns to tolerate handling, doesn't include friendship with humans, and so we can only watch them and wonder about their ancient and secret thoughts, learning even through them that beauty doesn't mean just the noble head of a fine horse, the beautiful eyes of a fawn, or the exquisite appeal of a flying squirrel. As beauty is in the water snake's sinuous flow of movement, in the hairy-legged spider's poised body, it is also in the awkward-gaited 'possum, with his leering mouth and ratlike tail, for like all creatures he is beautifully equipped for his way of life.

4.   Flying Squirrels

ONE EVENING IN AUGUST, just before closing time, a car drew up in front of the museum and several persons got out. When the driver opened the compartment at the rear of the car, everyone busily gathered around and watched them with growing interest and curiosity, speculating on what they would soon be bringing to the museum door. We knew that if it were a huge paper carton, it would most certainly be one small newborn bunny, because, almost invariably, little rabbits which could comfortably be carried in a small sack or box arrive in a large container. But these people seemed to be carefully picking up many small things and placing them in a small box.

There was quite a group to meet them when, after endless delay, they arrived at the museum door, and in the box were six tiny flying squirrels!

As they handed us the squirrels, they told us they had been taking apart an old bird house they had thought to be empty, when the six babies tumbled out and the mother dashed away in fright. Probably by evening the mother would have returned and moved them to a new nest if they had been placed in a grape basket and hung at the same place where the bird house had been, but we were pleased with our new additions — which tipped the druggist's scales at a mere four ounces altogether when we weighed them!

FLYING SQUIRRELS

As soon as I put my hand in the box, I began to understand why all of these people had been so busy picking them up and putting them down. The six little things clung to my fingers like woolly moths. By gently brushing them off, I only got them on the other hand, and in spite of their eyes being still sealed, their sprightly crawl made it very difficult to get them all in one place at the same time.

These were the tiniest youngsters I had yet tried to raise and I had little faith in success. The small tip of a medicine dropper was a clumsy and crude thing in their tiny mouths, but a bubble of milk is a bubble of milk to most babies and they eagerly gulped down a whole dropperful and fell asleep. We put them on a wool blanket placed over a hot-water bottle in a nest box. Within the next three or four days, their eyes came open, and shortly afterward, two of the five males died. The remaining three males and the single female grew to maturity.

As babies they resembled elfish creatures out of a Disney fantasy. While the flight of flying squirrels is not true flight, it is a long swooping glide made possible by the spreading of the furry and elastic membrane that extends between the front and hind legs along

each side of the body. Hidden in the fold of skin is a delicate cartilage attached only at the wrist; this serves, like a spoke in an umbrella, to support the flare of skin so that in flight the animal is almost square in shape. The flattened tail is thought to be of some use in putting on the brakes at the point where the animal makes a very short upward swoop to land against a tree trunk. The delicate membrane of these babies rippled and draped like a sort of nightshirt. Later, when the fur grew out thicker, the lines of the membrane were lost and hardly noticeable, but in those early weeks it was almost as if they had to grow into their strange garments of skin. Waking from sleep, they would yawn several times and stretch their tiny, silver paws far out in front of their noses, making a dolman sleeve effect of the membrane.

It was quite impossible to tell one from the other and so at the feedings — which took place every three hours — whoever was in charge simply slipped the fed ones down his shirt. Sometimes they lay there sleeping, but often they raced about as if they were in their own hollow tree. So from the beginning, the flyers became unafraid of handling by people, and for months afterward they would zip down one's shirt-front at the slightest alarm. It was rather startling to visitors when four little wide-eyed faces with enormous black eyes suddenly appeared between the buttonholes!

At about eight weeks of age the flyers outgrew their small nursery cage and their medicine-dropper feedings. They drank milk from a dish and began gnawing on nuts, grain, fruit, and vegetables. They were big enough to be transferred to a larger cage made of one-eighth-inch wire mesh over which their tiny feet traveled like lightning. Dry oak leaves and sawdust covered the floor, and the furnishings consisted of a large, hollow stump with a soft, woolly sweater at the bottom of it for a den, a running wheel with a diameter of nine inches for play and exercise, and some branches stretched across the cage in several directions.

Soon after the family moved in, a new little female about the same age was brought to Trailside. Flyers breed well in captivity and we hoped that one of the two females would have a litter. The following April, Midget, the new female, failed to appear for two evenings at feeding time, and, when dug out, was found huddled with three pink wriggling babies in the bottom of a much too small hollow log.

A private nursery cage was arranged and the family moved to it. For fear of her growing upset, we waited several days before looking into the nest. On the fifteenth day I risked taking them out of the nest. They were three males and weighed one ounce each. Plumper and more healthy youngsters I have never seen. They were twice the size of the original four which we had hand-raised, and yet they were only half as mature — which may mean that members of small families are larger at birth and grow faster.

At this age their bellies were quite bare of fur, the eyes still closed, and the tails showed no sign whatever of ever being flat like a feather. They were round and thick and pink like a bristly angleworm. At twenty-two days, their eyes opened and the babies were well furred all over. They could crawl just a bit too fast to keep track of. In the nest they could be seen scratching their ears and licking any faces that happened to be near-by as well as washing their own. Big-headed and blunt-faced, they resembled little Saint Bernard puppies. Midget, the mother, contrary to all accounts I have heard of mother flyers, was very ferocious about anyone putting a finger near the nest and was always on guard — ready to nip sharply. It was only at night, when she was at the food dish, that I could get a baby out of the nest before she attacked. At the age of thirty-nine days, the babies weighed two ounces each and it was impossible to distinguish who was who, although, as is usual in a litter, one showed a gentler disposition.

Swiftly they grew up, and in no time at all few of us could tell the young from the older animals except for their slightly more innocent expressions. In the three years that have passed since the original eight arrived, there have been several deaths and replacements. The total is again eight, but who they are is more than I can tell.

Actually now that they are older, we see very little of them. Their play time is at night, and except for an hour or so in the morning when they are active, they resent bitterly being disturbed during their daytime sleep. They even sleep harder than most animals, and when roused by day their dropping eyelids give them the sleepiest look I've ever seen on an animal face.

They waken at twilight. As the night grows older, they grow wilder and more active and their wheel spins with a loud whirring sound until dawn. I have never seen them play and tussle with each other as do the tree squirrels, but neither do they ever quarrel. Perhaps like flying fish their joy is to be flying about in each other's company. Yet, in spite of their seeming to pay little attention to one another, flying squirrels are generally found in the wild living together in large or small groups in hollow trees or even in the attic eaves of country houses. Some observers report that the twilight flight of large numbers of them from tree to tree seems mainly for the sheer delight in flight.

Of the present group, we have one favorite, distinguished perhaps because he is the tamest of the lot, and because he recognizes his name of Bug or Bugsie. He waits eagerly every morning at the door of the hollow stump when the cage-cleaning work brings me to the flyers' cage. As soon as the door of the cage is opened, he flies straight out as if on an invisible spring. After romping merrily all over me and into all of my pockets, he goes about his morning business which consists of trips to the kitchen nut supply and visits to my desk drawer, where he frequently finds a stray nut. Should I pass while he is at his mischief, he zips through the air and lands on me. When I meet him and snap my fingers, he leaps straight up from the floor and lands on my knee. Some mornings he spends riding back and forth on the food tray from the kitchen to the cages, helping himself to whatever pleases him. Occasionally in the evening I take him with me to a friend's house. This new experience never upsets him. He immediately invents a game, such as skittering up and down the long carpeted hall or bounding with wide leaps across the room, over the chairs and up the draperies. At last excitement wears him out and he curls up in a round ball where the draperies are gathered together at the top of the window and sleeps for the rest of the evening, with his flat little tail curled round his face to shut out the light.

It has been said that no American animal, not even the mild-appearing cottontail, is as gentle as the flying squirrel. A cage of young cottontails often show gashes and frayed ears, but I have never seen or heard a flyer quarrel with any strange flyer. I have found half-grown flyers difficult or impossible to tame, but their nips are only in self-defense when unused to handling.

They are capable of much courage — one amazing story is told of a mother moving her four young by making eight flying trips — a distance of eighty-six yards, across a river. She moved each one from a hat held by a man to her new den. Each take-off was from the top of a tree.

In my experience, none but the weasel among captive animals of this region has the elfish charm of the flyer and the air of being not of this world. Other squirrels are more affectionate and more capable of showing various moods, including anger, but none can equal the flyer for sheer joy of living and moving. Whatever he does, he does it as hard as he can and yet his gray sleekness is always unruffled, his snowy underparts are as white as newly laundered linen, his 'wing' folds are always neatly pressed, and his featherlike tail is always brushed and parted in the middle as if newly preened. If there were cherubs in the animal kingdom, they undoubtedly would have the faces and temperaments of flying squirrels.

5.

Trixie, The Gray Fox

TRIXIE'S PLEASED LITTLE BARKS as she paces slowly back and forth are like gay little Pan pipe notes. There is nothing frantic or restless in her pacing, it is slow and measured and each dainty foot is lifted high and placed with precision upon the same spots over and over again. Sinuously she swerves at the end of her cage, and all through the pacing her sharp barks are uttered.

The deaths of baby cottontails are highlights in Trixie's days. To her they are a choice morsel which her wild innards crave and require. She will eat them, every bit, fur and bones, but first she will pace back and forth in her night cage carrying them in her mouth. Sometimes, when she stops for a moment, someone speaks to her. Like the housecat with a mouse, she shows in every movement of her body as she begins to pace again that she is proud and pleased. Like a cat, too, sometimes she tosses the rabbit and deftly catches it or pounces on it with her tiny forepaws, remembering vaguely with some racial memory the mice she never caught. Although she comes of a long line of mousers of the highest skill,

35

Trixie never knew the wild and opened her eyes for the first time in a shoe box. 'Trixie's going home to her den!' you'll hear some boy say, because we always wonder if this pacing before the meal has something to do with the journey home after the kill.

But life in a shoe box, a year as a house pet, two years in a zoo and a year at Trailside did not entirely destroy the wild strain in Trixie. She is still a fox — alert, sharp-eared, quick as a flash to respond when some unexpected sound or movement startles her. There is a deep, throaty growl of warning when a hand rests on her back at a time when she is concerned with other sights and sounds.

Trixie is at her friendliest from March through August. Almost everyone who stops to talk to her or pet her during this time is rewarded by her doglike good humor. She flings herself on her back and warbles and yips in keen delight as she thumps her heavy tail. But she does have her favorites, who are, oddly enough, chosen at first sight and forever remembered as delightful persons. They may stroke her short, thick pepper-and-salt coat, scratch her creamy undersides, and rub her ears and shoulders, which are the soft rust-color of fallen pine needles. Trixie prefers persons of quiet bearing and invariably shows her most cordial moods to those who are on the heavy-set side! A few strangers are also recognized on sight as enemies, and it matters not to Trixie how attentive they are or how much they really wish to be friends. She will have none of them and shows her dislike by growls and bristlings. After the end of summer, she grows aloof and reserved, and although she accepts attentions she rarely sings even to her favorites until the following spring.

There isn't a great deal to tell about Trixie's personal life. She is just a beautiful gallant creature whose every motion is perfection and whose ways make one dream of the spirit of the wild and the deep forests where secluded trails are made only by the comings and goings of the fourfooted.

But while Trixie's own life is simple and uneventful, the long and colorful history of her race is written in her alert, sensitive ears, her delicate bones, her dark catlike eyes that show only a vertical

36

slit of pupil in bright light and dilate to a large, dark circle in the twilight. We have never seen Trixie climb a tree. No doubt she will die without knowing that experience, but holding her fine slender foot with its sharp, recurved claws, we can better understand how her kind, the gray foxes, are the expert climbers that they are, and have won the name of tree fox. Of all the foxes that can scramble from branch to branch until high in a tree, none can outclimb the grays.

On Trixie's indoor cage, used mostly at night, is a sign reading: 'Don't be surprised if you find a gray fox asleep in a hawk's nest sixty feet high in a tree top.' Not many of us are likely to be prowling about hawks' nests at that height, but no doubt many an idly flapping crow, hawk, or owl veers suddenly when he finds his favorite resting platform already occupied by the small, curled, tail-hidden body of a gray fox napping in the sunny top of a tall pine that rises some forty feet before the branches spring out from its trunk. How does she get there? Not by leaping lightly to a low branch and tacking back and forth as does the red fox, but by climbing straight up the sheer branchless trunk as a cat would. And once there, her small eight-pound body fits snugly in a large hawk's nest.

This nest may be one of her several hunting lodges scattered over her range and used on nights far from home, for the grays never sleep out in the open as the reds do. These occasional shelters may also be in hollow trees or logs or in the completely safe hide-out deep in a rocky crevice which is her first choice of a den for the three to six young born in May. Unlike the red fox who digs her den, the gray never goes to earth of her own digging.

When pursued by men and dogs, the grays always tree if possible and here so often meet their deaths. When shaken or stoned from the tree, the gray has many odds against him, for his powers of running are not to be compared with the red fox for endurance. Fresh dogs and horses run him down in about two hours. However, he has one trick left in the bag and many times has been able to outdodge rather than outrun his tormentors, because the gray fox,

in spite of short legs not built for speed, can swerve and twist and turn upon his tracks by means of his long rudderlike tail which serves as a balancer on sharp turns. It is the only fox tail that is keeled or flattened sidewise instead of being round and bushy. *Urocyon*, his Latin name, means flat-tailed. This tail is also the gray fox's identification badge. Its black tip places its owner in the gray fox group, which is not to be confused with the red fox group, which bears a white tail tip.

To others of his kind this tail can send a message full of meaning. All members of the fox, wolf, and coyote families bear a scent gland on the upper side of the tail located at the point where it is attached to the body. The size of this invisible gland varies in species and also somewhat in individuals, but the gland of the gray fox is the longest of them all, reaching almost to the tail tip. This gland is covered with hair known as the 'tail mane' and may easily be distinguished from the fur proper by its bristly hairy texture and the lack of downy underfur. In the coyote, for instance, the mane is but a small dab of dark fur, but in the gray fox it is an upstanding strip of black extending the length of the tail and joining the black tip. Ernest Thompson Seton has written at length on this interesting subject, and one may speculate on how the scent from this gland, instantly recognized by creatures of the same kind, can convey many messages. Wolves that hunt in packs undoubtedly make greater use of this primitive means of communication, for they have their meeting places, hunt the same territory, and cling together in family groups, whereas the fox runs only with its mate.

We've all been amused to watch the family dog spend a whole evening investigating our clothes or shoes after we have been in the woods or among strange dogs or other animals. Over and over he reads with his nose, drawing in long paragraphs, or should we say smellographs, of news, snuffing it out to clear his nostrils — only to go back again and again to re-read some particularly tantalizing bit. The left shoe may be of only faint interest while the right toe attracts him like a magnet, and yet he must go back and sniff of one's ankle time and again in order to piece this bit of information in with that toe business until the whole picture is as clear to him, no doubt, as if he had seen it with his own eyes, or rather smelled it with his own nose. And so we may imagine the gray fox coming home to his den, or resting on his favorite rocky ledge, and finding plainly written for any fox to read such messages as:

'Your old enemy is in the neighborhood. Beware!'

'The vixen you flirted with last week passed here this morning.'

'Me — I'm still a cub, but I know my way around.'

'Grandpa passed this way an hour ago, hot and tired, but he gave the dogs the slip.'

The body chemistry of that hot and tired animal has poured forth lively odors. Fear has distilled the invisible ink with which he wrote the message, perhaps by rubbing the surface of the gland against the rocks, as do the wolves, who use special rocks or tree trunks for their classified ad columns. The human nose can distinguish such strong odors as that of a frightened dog after a dog

fight. Even our dull sense of smell may pick up the strong flash
of odor which Trixie occasionally broadcasts when startled. This
is not difficult because the gray and his living quarters are normally
quite odorless, more so than many dogs — while the red fox is rank
with his own personal musk at all times.

The reputation of the gray is also in better odor than that of the
red fox, for although she will, of course, take hens and turkeys which
wander abroad and roost in the woods, she does not as a rule thieve
poultry from the farmyard or enter the locked henhouse by sheer
cunning. In fact, the gray is not considered cunning at all, and
may not only be trapped easily, but is often seen abroad, for it does
not avoid the sight of men, as the reds do. Baily tells of live-trap-
ping adult grays and having no difficulty in carrying them several
miles in his arms to the cage prepared for them. We have noticed
that no matter what her mood, Trixie never objects to being carried, but just because there is a chance that some day she might,
it is always one of the day's adventures.

Trailside days are never dull, although there are people accustomed to dealing with larger wilder animals in greater numbers
who naturally find chipmunks and deer mice small game. And
so it might rightly be said that life at Trailside is rather quiet, but
it is Trixie, the gray fox, who lends an exciting quality, however
small. Like Rover, the coyote, and Bambi, the fawn, who came
before her, Trixie is the uncertain, the unpredictable, the un-
fathomable. You may get this feeling by looking long into the
eyes of a tiny deer mouse, but it is more exciting to realize that you
have bridged, if only by a gossamer thread, the unlighted places
between this world and the world of a deer, a prairie wolf, or a fox.

Trixie lolling on the blue velvet couch during an evening visit
with humans, contentedly lapping her much-loved bread and milk,
wagging her tail in welcome, eyeing a squirrel on her cage with in-
difference or losing a bit of her dignity as she is carried under my
arm to and from her big outdoor cage — these domestic events and
acquired ways only serve to make us realize that we are sheltering
a guest from that alien world. We have gentled out of her spirit

many of her native ways, and sometimes we long to ship her far away to freedom that she has never known, but then we look at the picture from another angle and the perspective changes.

We see her admired and loved by many children and adults who long after Trixie is gone will remember the winning ways of a young vixen who warmed their hearts by showing them special recognition, when she preferred to lie with her head on their knees and lick their hands with her tiny pointed tongue. Daily she makes friends for her kind, and of these there cannot be too many. Her kind, like the jays, crows, starlings, hawks, weasels, owls, and wolves, are outcast among men because they live in the manner in which they were equipped to live — using their wit and strength to live and bear and feed their young. She will never have a mate, and the songs she sings to welcome us in the spring and summer are perhaps echoes of those her kind have sung to each other since the days before history. But only a thread links her to us and in between are the unlighted places. We know and love her so well. We know so very little about her.

6. Bird Royalty, The Barred Owls

'PUNCH? JUDY? PRINCE? How do you tell all three apart?' ask the Trailside visitors, as they stand beside the cage of barred owls. But this is a simple matter, considering how shepherds and farmers with their large flocks and herds can tell so many animals apart.

And so I say: 'Look closely. There's Punch, with his innocent, gentle face. Here's Judy, who is a bit fiercer and less trusting, and has close-set eyes. Prince there seems older somehow, and though not as trusting as Punch, he is not as fierce as Judy.' Each owl face, with its eyes brown as forest pools, has a different message. Every time you look, you get the message and there's no mistaking whom it is from.

Punch never knew the wild, as he was hand-raised. The other two came to Trailside when they were full-grown hunters. Both have broken wings, now healed, but useless for prolonged flight. For the better part of five years these great birds of prey have sat

42

placidly in their outdoor cage watching, with a mild curiosity, but a keen eye, the activities about the museum, accepting captivity with no outward struggle and apparently little inner conflict.

Perhaps that is the wisdom of owls. They are so philosophic about the whole thing. Supremely indifferent to environment, resigned without being hopeless, accepting when they choose to, but not open to force. These are royal captives who are more in the nature of hostages than creatures merely deprived of their freedom. And my own sense of their royal heritage is present in all of my dealings with them.

I took Judy from a garage, where for several days she had been resisting the cautious efforts of the owner to persuade her to leave. Back at the museum, I found that her wing was broken. She sat on my knee as I examined it, and the sharply severed bones punctured my fingers as I tried to fit them together. But Judy only sat and stared at me curiously. There was never a flinch or change of expression. Not once did she pull back or flutter an eyelid. Why? Physical distress in owls is doubtless not connected with mere broken bones. Judy removed her bandage and splint three times and in the end the wing had to be allowed to heal unset.

Punch was picked up, with a broken wing and no tail feathers, in a field. He was quite exhausted after a battle with a flock of crows who were making the most of the rare advantage of finding an old enemy disabled and at their mercy.

Hunger, too, in these birds seems to be taken as a matter of course. There was a period of ten days one winter when not a single chicken head was to be had, owing to a widespread shortage of fowl. During that time the owls did not eat. Horse meat, liver, and dead rabbit did not tempt them. At last, when the chicken heads arrived, we all rushed out to feed them at midday. Punch, Judy, and Prince sat in perfect dignity, and like all self-respecting owls waited until dusk to break their fast.

On a steady diet of two chicken heads a day, they renew their feathers and stay in beautiful plumage. This seemingly small appetite is not difficult to understand when you examine the body of a barred owl. He stands eighteen to twenty inches high, a square, chunky, fat-appearing bird compared in size to a twenty-inch beaver, but under the fluffy feathers of the body and the large wings is a mere doll's body that is mostly legs. Altogether he weighs from one to two pounds!

Like so many tame wild creatures, owls are fascinating because one is never quite sure how they are going to receive a friendly gesture. It is always necessary to approach them with a certain degree of courtesy to match their own gentle dignity. They like to have you speak politely and say hello before you open their cage to enter. They are much reassured by a soft voice, which they will answer by a light *tap, tap* of their big hooked beaks. When threatening, they snap their beaks, but this loud sound is sharply different from the friendly *tap, tap* that is accompanied by the slow blink of the great dark eyes as the china-blue film of opaqueness that is the 'third eyelid' passes slowly across them. The mildness of the barred owls is found only in the rather small eye of the barn or monkey-faced owl. Almost all other owls have glowing amber eyes.

Five years ago when Punch first arrived, he was not quite full-grown. I had never seen a barred owl face to face, and although now he looks to me like nothing so much as a barred owl, at that time I could think only of a great brown-eyed cat whenever I looked at him. Sitting on the floor of a small indoor cage, he peered at every part of his new surroundings and talked endlessly in a pleasant but questioning voice that was for all the world like the soft meowings of a cat.

Punch, Judy, and Prince still make 'cat talk.' Sometimes they greet you with it. Usually they will answer your own imitation of it. *Waa, waa, waa, waa* they question back. The only translation I can think of that would begin to express the polite curiosity of this owl word would be the German word *bitte*. I have never heard our owls talking among themselves with these words — they seem only to be used to or before human friends. Maybe they do not say it to me at all. Perhaps they are merely commenting to each other about me. No matter — they seem to understand my imitation of it, and it is always interesting to find them alert and on guard, momentarily forgetful of our old friendship, and then to make 'owl talk' with them and see their ruffled feathers settle down into place, their eyes grow dreamy, and the blue film pass slowly back and forth across their eyes. Then is the time when you may raise your hand and begin to scratch an owl's head. Like most birds who are not too fearful to relax, they dearly love having their heads scratched, and will sit with their chins almost on their feet so low do they bend over, jibbering softly to themselves in a high-pitched quaver.

I say *you* because anyone can scratch an owl's head, provided he follows the routine and makes no false move. More and more I think that is a part of the secret of bird and animal handling. They respond to one person because they are used to his ways and words. Creatures of habit, both birds and animals become terror-stricken when a change is made. So long as everything, every move and sound, proceeds in the expected manner they feel reasonably sure of what to expect. A different grip, an unsure manner, a lack of confidence in approach and handling, and the bird or animal becomes unmanageable with fright. He cannot trust someone who cannot trust himself.

I will never forget the first time that I found an owl's ears as I scratched his head. They are two great holes low down near the beak, with large flaps standing out in front of the ear opening. They are clean and pink and delicate as a shell and the feather arrangements on the rims are marvels to behold, but not so beautiful as those that overlay the eyelids. With such wonderful organs of hearing, it is small wonder that the owl skimming on soundless feathers through the woodlane can catch the tiniest squeak of a mouse or shrew or the velvet footfall of a rabbit and pounce upon them for the kill without their ever being aware of what struck. I suppose no one has seen him hunting with his 'ears peeled,' but certainly they must stand wide open, and perhaps the front flap is for ready closing should he brush a branch as he strikes the ground.

Half of the mystery surrounding the owl is the silence of his flight. It is not a case of his flight being more quiet than that of other birds. It is absolutely soundless. Many times while I was raking their cage, the owls have flown over my head, and only the thump of their feet landing on the opposite perch warned me that they had changed positions.

Unlike crows, pigeons, hawks, ducks, or roosters whose stiff wing feathers cut the air with a sharp whistle, the owl has feathers downy as a moth's wing. A velvet nap covers the upper surface of the large quills and fringes their margins. Wind resistance against this smooth downy surface is practically nothing. Hence the silence, compared to the whistle produced by air passing over the ribbed contour of the ordinary feather.

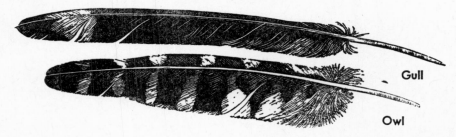

Gull

Owl

There are such interesting answers to any question about birds and animals that one really misses a great deal by not hunting for the answer. Almost everyone laughs hilariously when the solemn owl screws his head around so far that he is looking down his back, but hardly anyone wonders what the real reason is for this strange habit. Have you ever noticed an owl rolling those great eyes and looking from side to side or out of the corner of his eye at you? Of course not, simply because he cannot do it. His eyes are fixed in a bony rim. In order to see what is not straight before him, he must turn his whole head. Besides having eyes that won't move, owls are the only birds with eyes that face to the front. The owls hunt the side-eyed birds and animals, such as mice and rabbits, squirrels and other vegetable-eaters. Hunted folk usually eat green stuff. They needn't look at what they eat once they get it in their paws, but they need always to be on the alert, watching out on both sides and sometimes over their shoulder so that hunting folk won't get them too easily. And the hunting folk, the meat-eaters, such as the hawks, dogs, wolves, foxes, cats, owls, and men, have front eyes in order to follow their prey ahead of them.

Almost everyone must unlearn some mistaken idea about every animal. Most persons believe that all owls are blind by day. This is founded on hearsay. Like the eyes of a cat or a fox, theirs are constructed so that the iris of the eye parts like a curtain allowing the greatest amount of light to strike the pupil when the light is scarce at dusk and dawn, the hours for good hunting. In total darkness they are, of course, as blind as you or I would be, but as long as there is some light they can make the most of it and therefore see more clearly than the rest of us with our pupils that are unable to dilate.

Owls do a lot of simple staring by day, because there are few animals about to arouse them to hunger and the kill. But Punch and Judy and Prince are quick to notice such novel things as a pair of white shoes among a crowd of otherwise black-shod visitors. Small movements on the ground cause them to peer down curiously. They also watch the door of the museum and bob their heads up and down, eager to see what or who is coming out next.

One of the nicest illustrations of their ability to see and recognize strange occurrences happened while they were on exhibit at a nature conference on the mezzanine floor of a large Chicago hotel. Of course, they were fairly bursting with wonder at the strange surroundings, but being used to crowds they gradually seemed to decide that these were only people after all and not much different from the people they were accustomed to have stare at them. So they fluffed out and stared back.

I had been keeping my eyes glued on them, as they were going through their first experience of being away from home and legleashed to a perch without a cage. I turned away for a moment and when next I looked I was startled to see the change. They were one-half as narrow and seemed twice as tall as they had been a minute before and as they peered over the heads of the crowd, they seemed to grow taller every second. The crowd parted and I saw what had frozen them so — six little Indian boys in full regalia came single file down the floor. I regret to say that they did not stop to visit our owls whose heads turned to view them until they were out of sight. Then only did Punch and Judy begin to relax from their 'old stick' appearance and to assume the comfortable fluffy at-home attitudes. I won't go so far as to say that they recognized an ancient enemy. Perhaps they even got the unfamiliar scent of buckskin, fox tail, and eagle feathers. At any rate, they saw something different in the crowd, and until they were sure the possible danger was past, they weren't going to be caught fluffy and conspicuous up on a perch in plain sight. So they did the owlish thing and made themselves tall, thin, and rigid — hoping to be mistaken for an old lichen-covered stub of a tree branch. Their instincts didn't fail them.

The barred owls manage to preserve their dignity even when they are soaking wet and appear to be frightful caricatures of themselves. Bathing they delight in, although they emerge looking like some queer old men from Mars. We spray them daily with the garden hose and they turn from side to side raising each wing so that no part of their thin, sinewy bodies shall be missed, or they sit placidly on their shelves with closed eyes as the water showers over them. If the day is very hot, they leap down to the cage floor and dance about in the spray with that laughable rocking gait. At last, when thoroughly bedraggled, several unsuccessful efforts must be made before they are able to flop and clamber up to their perches to sit with the water running from their beaks.

For the last several years they have spent the winter months indoors sitting in the window of a large screened-off alcove in the basement of the museum. With this arrangement what little food they eat doesn't freeze, and they themselves must be much more comfortable than if they were just to sit without exercising for so many wintry months. For these six months they hoot a great deal. Somehow I never tire of hearing them. No one enters the drive on foot or by car after nightfall that they do not sound the alarm and in between they hoot for the fun of it and answer my hooted greetings each time I come down the basement stairs. There are some evenings when the darkened museum sounds like a parliament of fowls, for the cooings of ring doves and mourning doves follow close upon the wild free cries of the owls in the basement — and of course my own imitations of them all, as I continue to try in vain to reproduce accurately those odd intakes of breath and throaty burblings.

It was always a great blessing to Trailside that Rover, our pet coyote, never found in the hoot of the owls that particular note that set him howling in his beautiful high soprano voice. The air-raid siren was irresistible to him and certain junior assistants were also entrusted with the right pitch. But fortunately for him, police and fire-engine sirens were forbidden in our village about the same time that he began to get in voice, so his concerts were privately arranged and took place behind closed windows and for a selected audience. He performed only on request.

Our owls have three distinct calls. Punch will readily hoot in your face, and so I am sure of his. Translated into words and notes it is: *ah whah, wa, wa, wa, wa, wa, wa, wa . . . ah whah!* — the seven *wa's* rising in pitch with a sharp *ah whah* at the end, reminiscent of the sailor's *ahoy* in accent and inflection. Judy and Prince never hoot when one is present, and so I have not placed the origin of the other two calls. One is roughly similar to a loud yawn — *ah whah!* The other is *hoo hoo, hoo hoo, hoo hoo, hoo hoo, hoo hoo, hooooooo.* These two calls are distinctly different, and either or both may have given rise to the name of eight-hooter, by which the barred owls are often called. And only once have I heard a visitor hoot at the owls in their own language. He was a lad from the country. I made sure to find out how he knew the call so well. The owls must have been dumbfounded at having someone who really knew what he was hooting about. They did not answer, however, for when in the outdoor cage they rarely hoot by day. Their night calls are confined to the colder months during which pairing takes place.

50

BIRD ROYALTY, THE BARRED OWLS

In giving his call, Punch puffs out the feathers of his throat and those around his beak making an old-fashioned beard-and-mustache effect. The grandest gesture of the barred owls is their rarely seen on-guard pose. A strange dog approaching the cage at night is generally cowed into retreat when what he supposes to be roosting chickens turn into magnificent warriors presenting a four-foot spread of sheer wing expanse. The wings stretched to their farthest are raised with the outer surfaces to the front, forming a backward-reaching curve that meets above the lowered head. Cautiously 'the birds teeter and turn this way and that, always keeping the enemy presented with this terrifying and slow-moving shield of feathers which they manage with the fascinating skill of the peacock or gobbler with spread tail.

The more I know of owls in captivity, the more I am impressed by their soundness and stability of character, expressed in poise, dignity, gentleness. These more gracious traits in their make-up have no quarrel with the fierce predatory flashes that lie so little beneath the surface calmness. 'A little strength must whip hard, great strength need not whip at all' . . . that, to me, expresses the great owls. Within memory, their bodies were commonly nailed to barn doors by unenlightened farmers. Now they are protected in many states and share with other predators the refuge at Hawk Mountain in Pennsylvania — the first and only area set aside for the protection of great birds of prey. May their tribe increase! not only because of their value in making a tardy check on the small rodents whose numbers have so increased since men have waged war upon predators, both bird and animal, but because they are a part of the scheme of things in a world where creatures of grandeur and savage beauty are dwindling too fast.

7.

Loki, The Hob Polecat

WHEN OUR POLECAT ARRIVED, he was given the name Loki because he belongs to the weasel clan, and that — by our human standards — has all of the unhappy traits possessed by Loki, mischief-maker of the Norse Gods. The weasel clan is a large one. Most of the valuable fur-bearers are found in it, and its dominant traits are stamped with clear-cut elegance on almost every member of it. There are the weasels whose smallest member is the Least Weasel — only six or seven inches in length — that turns snow-white in winter and is fit for the fairy queen to ride. There are the water-loving minks, the rarely seen martens, the highly prized sables and ermines. There are the fishers who feast upon porcupines and suffer no trouble from their quills, the squat but swiftly digging badgers, the otters of land and the rare sea otters, the ferrets, so closely akin to the polecats, but whose real origin as a domesticated animal has been lost. There is the magnificent wolverine whose fur is used by Northern trappers to line their parka hoods, because it has the mysterious quality of not collecting the frozen breath of the wearer when in sub-zero temperatures. These are but the most well-known of the tribe.

LOKI, THE HOB POLECAT

There are no timid souls in the weasel clan. All of its members are hunters, except the skunk. The skunk is the animal most persons think of when the word polecat is mentioned, but the skunk is strictly an American animal. The true owner of the name 'polecat' is European. Because they are related and like each other in some ways, the name 'polecat' was given to our American skunk by early natural history observers in America, just as the name 'buffalo,' a strictly old-world animal, was given to his cousin the American bison.

Although members of the weasel tribe vary in size from a few ounces to thirty-five pounds and include tree-dwellers, walkers of the earth, burrowers within it, water creatures, and those that are equally at home both in the water and on land, they all bear strong family likenesses.

The polecat has the long, sinewy shape and the alert sharp face and temperament of the ferrets, weasels, and minks. His peculiar scent places him definitely in this great tribe which old nature writers called the 'stinkards.' Loki lives in a cloud of his own perfume which appeals differently to different people. All boys seem to think that it is rather pleasant. When they come home with it clinging to their sweaters — and it does cling for many hours — their mothers fail to appreciate the beauty of it. To me it is something like the fragrance of very strong honey, and it also has the pungency of a bed of sweet alyssum on a hot summer's day. There perhaps I am prejudiced, but I am sorry that the publishers could not make it possible for this one page to be scented with the very interesting odor of Loki's fur so that you could know just what it is like most of the time.

Pain, anger, and excitement will cause all of these animals to throw off a very powerful and unpleasant scent. It was only in the first days of his life at Trailside that Loki showed his alarm in this manner. Since then we have noticed that it is only in November that Loki advertises that he is a polecat, and although at this time his personal brand of perfume may be attractive to other polecats, it is most unpleasant to human noses. Fortunately it fades away in about twenty minutes, as it hasn't the staying qualities of the skunk's scent.

It was this personal odor which placed the European polecat among the animals hunted by hounds in France and England until a generation or so ago. It was said that he was one animal that was killed first and hunted afterward, since after the kill the strongly scented trail could lead the hounds in a wide circle and back to the dead body again. The polecat's straight course, unlike the zigzag trail of the stoat or weasel, added to his attractiveness as a quarry and some hunts lasted as long as seven or eight hours. In those days he was called the 'foumart,' a shortening of the term 'foul marten,' in contrast to the pine marten who lacked the strong scent and was called the sweet marten. But both were pursued as vermin by hunters, game wardens, and farmers. The hounds trained to the work were called 'foumart' hounds or just 'mart' hounds. In the past mart hunts were a favorite sport in the Lakeland region of England, where it was a custom to present the skin of the foumart, worth a half crown, to the poorest man of the hunt.

From these old days, too, dates the quaint little titles of Hob and Gill designating the male polecat from his lady. From January until mid-May it was open season on the hobs and their gills, March, April, and May being considered the months of best hunting. But in May and June, the wedding months, the foumarts were allowed to retire to their dens, which was known as a 'bield,' to rear their family of three to five young ones. The bield might be under a barn or a heap of stones or even in a drain. Often it was near water, for polecats favor frogs and eels on their diet list and are excellent swimmers when tempted by these choice items of food.

Because of his larger size the polecat can kill larger animals than his weasel cousin. But he is not quite so bloodthirsty a hunter as the weasel, who has never been known to eat anything other than raw animal food. The polecat will eat fruits and rob beehives to satisfy his sweet tooth. He is, however, equally skilled in the art of killing, not only for food, but killing, so it is said, for the sheer pleasure of killing. Perhaps we might call him and his cousins the 'sportsmen' of the animal world!

It was a snowy day in November when Loki arrived at Trail-side. He had been treed by coon dogs whose owner climbed up to bring down what he naturally thought was a coon and found Loki whose identity had him guessing. Loki must have been living in the wild for some time, as he was in fine condition, although his teeth showed that he was no longer a young animal. The thick coat of brown-tipped guard hairs, with an underfur of rich yellow-orange, stood on end with that beautiful electric vitality of the healthy animal when living an active outdoor life. Doubtless he had escaped from someone recently, as he was quite easy to handle, but even after he was thoroughly accustomed to being handled he would snap when some boy held him close to his head. This we imagined was instinct prompting him to bite at hair or fur and find out afterward whether or not there was an animal under it.

Owing, no doubt, to his advanced age, he was anything but true to his new name Loki. He was always able to outsleep even an opossum. For his size he can eat a greater variety of food and more of it than any of our other pets and furthermore he always cleans up his plate. He has no off days when food isn't interesting. He likes it cooked and raw; he likes fruit and vegetables and bread and milk and honey just as well as he likes raw meat or a live mouse or snake. Loki even likes his cage and never scrabbles to get out. He simply eats and sleeps and smells. Nothing upsets him except a delay in the serving of his meals.

For all of his sleepy ways, he is an amusing little creature. When disturbed he bobs up from his box and peers about as if to say, 'Who, me?' and then settles down to sleep again unless food is forthcoming. He can be propped up in a corner of his sleeping-box, where he slumps like a rag doll, and when picked up he is the perfect pet for holding. Anyone can hold Loki. He was born for it, although he never begs for attention. His sense of humor is his most endearing trait. Once on the floor he pays no attention to

you whatsoever, but begins a monotonous nosing about in dark corners and travels wherever possible along walls and under things unless you insist that he clown. Nonsense talk and a few passes with your hand as if you were trying to catch him will start a very gay and silly performance. With open mouth, as if he were laughing silently, he cavorts sidewise with humped back in mock haste until he falls over on his back several times. Then he struggles up on his short legs and bounces away backward like a wound-up toy. When you cease to tease, he goes on about his business as if you didn't exist. Loki is as silent as a rabbit about his play, but I have seen other polecats who played in this manner and made two sounds very similar to those of a weasel, a strange hiss and a rapid high-pitched humming.

Although Loki can't be trusted near other animals, he is the only one of our pets who can be allowed to take a walk out-of-doors without a leash. Round and round among the trees in the field near-by he will wander with you and he is always easy to catch and keep track of. He seems to have forgotten his ability to climb. Sometimes he finds a garter snake sunning along the old stone wall and then he is no longer a sleepy, domesticated pet. With one pounce and shake he has not only caught it, but has started to devour it. Lately his once sharp fangs have begun to grow blunt and discolored, showing signs of advancing age. He must be all of eight years of age or more.

Lovable Loki, although he is not found in the Forest Preserves and is not even native to America, is along with the skunk the best representative that Trailside could have of this large family of Mustelidae, many of which grow restless and frantic in captivity if they survive at all. Together these two illustrate an interesting story of the law of compensation in nature. The wild skunks for whom even the bears politely step aside possess that marvelously effective double-barreled scent gun under the tail which can fire some six feet or more. Because of this the skunk has little need for the keen sight, speed, and cunning needed by many animals for defense or food-getting. But lacking them the skunk must take his food where he finds it. A skunk's diet is made up of such things as the grubs and insects that he can dig out of rotted logs, the buried eggs of snapping turtles, the young of the birds which nest upon the ground, litters of field mice and newborn rabbits, frogs, crayfish, and even fruit and berries. While the polecat, the weasel, and the mink, all of which possess the power of throwing off a strong fetid odor when angered or injured, are unable to aim and fire at their enemies, consequently all of their resources are well developed, their native cunning and blood-thirstiness are aided by a keen sense of smell, hearing, and sight. Their slim, lithe shapes are suited for entering small burrows of chipmunks and ground squirrels and other creatures. They have often been seen attacking animals much larger than themselves.

There are days when Loki appears to be ill and feeble. He wanders about the floor aimlessly, and it is often some time before all of his short little legs begin to limber up and stay where he puts them. We sigh and wonder how soon it will be when some morning Loki doesn't waken to the scrape of the cage-cleaning tools and the jingle of keys.

John, the big white rabbit, sits in the middle of the floor staring pink-eyed into the wintery morning. Loki patters along the wall, uncertain of gait, looking old and weary. The minor complaints of the aged have come to plague him. He has just got over a case of lump jaw, which is an abscess about the head or neck that frequently troubles ferrets and polecats. Now and then he stops and stretches out in his tracks in weariness. Suddenly while I was blinking my eyes it happened. White fur flies; the long toenails of the rabbit scrabble at the floor as he dodges and tumbles and shakes loose the fury that has attacked him and skids out of the room to safety. Loki, looking smug, trots along the wall with an air of renewed zest in life. John is found trembling and wide-eyed, more frightened than hurt, though one ear shows a tiny red tooth hole. Frankly we are pleased when our little old hob polecat manages to make a mark on a victim. At the same time we try not to have it happen. But sometimes it is the guinea pig, sometimes the opossum whose cage is left open unintentionally and sometimes the white rabbit is caught off guard. Loki's sudden flares of latent strength and ferocity mean that he isn't so old and weary as he seems. We are glad that he still has the valiant spirit to try to do what Nature equipped him to do in life.

Turtles Here and There

8.

BOYS AND GIRLS everywhere like turtles. There is no reason to suppose that this is something new. Wherever there have been boys and girls and turtles, they have somehow got together. In Sicily, some two hundred years before Christ was born, some schoolboys stopped to play near a brickyard. Fresh and moist, the large bricks lay waiting to be baked. Then, as now, there was nothing so tempting as a place where one might scribble and so they inscribed on the wet, clay bricks three special words which tell a short but complete and familiar story. The words were 'turtle,' 'mill,' and 'pail.' The millponds and the pails in which boys those days carried home their turtles have all changed, but the boy and the turtle remain very much the same.

Actually, the turtle has been just about the same for the past one hundred and seventy-five million years, and through all of those years it has worn most of its skeleton on the outside instead of on the inside of its body, as other backboned animals do. Its kind has seen the greatest reptiles of all, the dinosaurs, come and go. The turtle has taken a place in the folklore of the Orient and in that of the American Zuñi Indian, but its greatest fame has always been its high place in the esteem of boys and girls everywhere. No one dislikes turtles as they sometimes dislike snakes or toads or frogs. When someone puts a turtle in your hand and says, 'Look, shall I show you my turtle?' you have somewhat the same feelings as you would if he were to show you a beautiful seashell, a smooth green stone, or a quaintly carved and painted good-luck charm.

Truly there is a charm about turtles that brings up feelings and thoughts no other creature can arouse. They are made to fit the hand, at least the little ones fit little hands, and the big ones fit big ones, except, of course, those rather monstrous snappers which weigh twenty or thirty pounds.

Children from away back in prehistoric days have had toys and pets. If the dog was the first wild creature to make his home in early man's cave dwelling, then turtles must have been among the very first pets collected by the child who played about the mouth of the cave. Perhaps the turtle has a special appeal because it comes very close to being a combination toy and pet, but like any toy or pet it should be handled with care.

Since our Trailside turtles are no different from the ones you find and keep for pets, I am going to discuss turtles in general and describe living conditions best suited to them, rather than describe the ones which come and go in our museum. A cold-blooded animal such as the turtle is not one whose blood runs cold nor does the term mean that these creatures feel no pain when mistreated. Cold-blooded means simply that their temperature is the same as their surroundings. Where winters are cold, they must hibernate beneath the pond bottom or in the ground to escape severe cold. In the hot summer they must not be kept in the hot sunlight without a chance to seek shelter in the shade. Remember this when you place your pets in the sun. Sometimes what seems to be merely pleasant sunshine to you is extreme heat to the turtle when you consider the reflection from the porch floor or the sidewalk where you may have placed your turtle's tank.

Turtles spend much of their time in the same position. For this reason they are so much more attractive and doubtless more at home when care and thought are given to their housing. This is not always possible nor practical — but in the case of very small turtles it is only a matter of providing the material and arranging it. One or two may be kept in a covered terrarium tank for some time before their crawling about makes it necessary to replace the damaged plants or moss. A good-sized clam shell or a small container is large enough to hold water which should be changed daily or as often as the black dirt discolors it. Leathery-leaved myrtle plants from the garden and philodendron vines from the five-and-ten draped over a bare branch thrive well in a terrarium, while stones and small gnarled roots add interest to the miniature scene. Feeding, which must take place underwater, is best done by removing the turtles to a separate pan of water. New arrivals sometimes do not feed as readily as those longer in captivity and even the good feeders are often upset and fail to eat when the feeding arrangements to which they are accustomed are suddenly changed.

If you prefer to keep turtles in a tank of water, a large collection of baby turtles can be housed in an aquarium 12 by 12 by 24 inches. A light concealed in a metal cover which is box-shaped or arched not only shows them off well, but keeps the temperature of the water and air from chilling. Water turtles should always have rocks or logs in the tank so that they can climb up and dry off. The best choice of roots or gnarled branches and logs are those of weathered driftwood without bark, smoothed by the action of sun, wind, and water. You can find them along the beaches. Charred wood that has been wave-tossed adds interest with its rich, black color, and does not discolor the water as do fresh branches collected from the woods. Aquarium gravel or pea-sized pebbles are the most practical for the bottom of the tank, as they may be scalded and used over and over again. However pleasing the white beach sand may be in the beginning, it soon grows dark and odorous if used for very long.

Turtles nibble and destroy growing water plants, but the green touch may be added by hanging philodendron vines in small glass bottles at the top of the tank so that they drape down almost to the water level. A permanent rockwork affair may be arranged by cementing rocks together and leaving a depression, up out of the reach of the turtles, where a rooted plant may grow undisturbed. But since green stuff is necessary in the diet of most water turtles by all means place some in the water occasionally. Tiny turtles clambering through the leaves of a green plant underwater make a delightful picture. A hardy and attractive land plant which also thrives underwater is moneywort. It grows in many rock gardens and often escapes to the wild. Gather a number of the vines, tie them together and weight with lead, and bury the tied stems in the gravel. It will last for some time before it needs replacing.

Among young turtles three of the hardiest and best eaters seem to be baby snappers, musks, and soft-shell turtles, with their long pointed snouts and olive-green fleshy backs shaped like pancakes. Make sure that the fast-growing snappers and soft shells are very small, because as soon as they are strong enough they attack and eat milder species, such as the Painted and the Troost's turtle. Young musk turtles are safe from these cannibals because of their bad odor.

The Troost's turtle, a Southern kind which sometimes bears a red cheek patch, is the one most often sold in pet shops or as a souvenir with an ugly coat of paint on its shell. If you very carefully flake off the paint with a dull knife blade, underneath you will find a beautifully marked green-and-brown shell. Paint interferes with the growth of the shell and disfigures a living creature which no paint could possibly improve.

Young turtles living in a large tank and accustomed to being fed in it learn quickly to recognize the approach of food and will crowd to be first with outstretched neck and watchful eye. In feeding, remember that a natural diet is always best. Give them as much of it as possible. Earthworms, small smooth caterpillars, insects, very tiny crayfish and other crustaceans, tadpoles, small fish dead or alive, and anything living that your net brings up from the pond or stream will be a healthful addition to their diet. When you cannot get a good supply of living things, give them bits of raw meat or fish cut so small that they can eat it in one or two gulps. Large pieces that need to be torn apart foul the water and uneaten bits of meat cause a very unpleasant odor. Careful feeding two or three times a week keeps the water clean. Ant eggs, as they are called in pet supply shops, are really the cocoons of ants with the dried bodies of other tiny creatures, and are eaten by turtles when nothing else is offered — but they are a poor diet at best.

Young turtles, and especially the Troost's, very frequently develop swollen eyes, probably because of something lacking in their diet in captivity. It is rarely possible to correct this by diet or sunlight. Even full-grown box turtles often suffer from sealed or swollen eyelids in the winter when their vitality is low. Occasionally this condition may be remedied by bathing the eyes in warm water until the lids soften and then gently pressing out the cheesy secretion which gathers under the lids. A good eyewash is one teaspoonful of borax and one of boric-acid powder dissolved in a pint of boiling water and used, of course, only lukewarm.

Large or full-grown turtles present a greater problem for attractive housing than the smaller ones. Snappers and musks, which are so attractive and active when tiny, grow rather unlovely as they get older and both may become very unpleasantly scented. They are forever hungry and eat large quantities of raw meat. They have a great deal more exposed flesh than other turtles and their legs, necks, and plastrons or lower shells constantly shed rags of gray skin which soon clouds the water of the tank. Both have an unhappy way of looking neglected when they are thriving.

In contrast to them is the very lovely spotted turtle. The spotted never grows much longer than four and one-half inches. The clean-scaled skin of the legs and throat is richly tinted with a bright peach color and the smooth, dark shell is spotted with yellow. I don't know of another species which seems so intelligent and inquiring. Its clear brown eyes gaze up at you with a knowing look and it will readily feed from your fingers. The spotted turtle should be displayed in a clear tank under a light, with dark logs for resting places in order to show up its streamlined beauty.

Box turtles of any size or species are all that turtles should be. It is rare to find a young one, but when tiny they are among the perfect creatures in nature. Middle-sized ones are a satisfying handful and big ones have a wise and ancient philosophical air which, added to their various facial expressions, gives them more personality than any other species. A fleshy hinge near the front of the plastron or lower shell makes it possible for the box turtle to snap the front and back edges of the lower shell tight against the upper. After hissing to expel the breath, the head, legs, and tail are drawn inside. The box is then shut tight and for some time the turtle is able to do without breathing and like a little armored tank resists its enemies.

Box turtles are believed to live from forty-five to one hundred and twenty-three years of age. The males grow larger than the females. Most adult specimens, with plastrons or undershells more than five and one-half inches in length, are males. The claws of the hind foot are shorter and thicker and his eyes are usually pink or bright red, while the female may have dark red, brownish-gray, or purplish eyes. However, this is not a sure proof of sex. Females have a flat or bulged lower shell, while the males have a slight arch toward the rear of the plastron.

Since the box turtle is a land creature, it eats out of water, and you may as well set the food before him and go away, because very often he says a long grace before he eats — although some will feed eagerly from the hand. Along with snappers, the box turtle seems to bear out the claim that turtles are not color blind. Red polish on the fingernails causes them to aim for the fingernails and to ignore the banana or other light-colored food offered in place of the accustomed raw meat. Along with quantities of raw meat, box turtles are fond of fresh ripe fruit, berries of all kinds, bananas, tomatoes, mushrooms, cantaloupe, watermelon, insects, earthworms, snails, and sometimes even soft bread.

Outdoor pens should have a sandy floor and wire mesh on all

six sides and wide molding board around the base on the inside of the pen to prevent them from climbing the wire and falling. A shallow pan of water for drinking and soaking is also necessary, as well as a sun shelter of some kind.

As soon as the days grow darker and colder, most older turtles in captivity will become much less active. Instinct urges the box turtle to begin to dig down a few inches a day to the depth of one or two feet below where the ground freezes and to spend the long winter months in a deep and deathlike sleep in which the flame of life burns very low. This is hibernation. In captivity there can be no true hibernation, but the chilly air causes the turtle to move less often and more slowly. Most of his time is spent motionless and in a dark corner or under leaves if his cage contains them. If he has been out in the sun and well fed all summer, he will continue to allow himself to be coaxed to eat about once a week, particularly if the meal is a generous one of bright red raw hamburger. However, after a good summer, a turtle is able to survive three months of winter fasting without hibernating.

In the wild the land turtles generally dig down into the ground, though some take to the pond like the water turtles, who usually bury themselves in the muddy bottom under the water. In the spring when the ice breaks up, the turtles rise once again to the surface. They will clamber up on some narrow log until it holds as many as will fit along its length, there to bake the winter chill from their bones. Don't capture one that first spring day. Wait a while — give him a chance to limber up and eat his fill of the first food his stomach craves after so deep a sleep and so long a hunger.

Dunder,
The Rat,

9.

and Blitzen, The Rabbit

SPRING AT TRAILSIDE is the time of violets, spring beauties, and cottontail babies. A whole month in the life of a cottontail has less action and interest than one day in the life of a squirrel. But everyone loves little cottontails just for being cottontails, with their large, innocent eyes, delicate ears, and powder-puff tails.

The earliest babies to arrive at Trailside in the spring are the cottontails, soft and gray as pussywillows, which might easily have been called 'bunny willows,' for it is the baby cottontails who crouch with ears laid back and feet tucked under in the shape of the willow catkins before they bloom.

The bunnies come to Trailside by ones, twos, and threes, by tens and thirteens. They arrive tucked into boxes, baskets, hats, and pinafores. One lovely spring day three of the most outsize football players I have ever seen face to face stalked into the museum in full regalia. As I was accustomed mostly to little people, it was something of a surprise to find the wide door blocked by these

67

three huge figures, but the real shock came when each extended a hand in which huddled a week-old cottontail. These bunnies will always seem the smallest that I have ever seen, but doubtless it was mere optical illusion. The boys had broken up their game and walked a good two miles to bring them to me when the nest was destroyed on the practice field.

Many of these babies that end up in the Trailside cottontail nursery are orphaned because their mother nested in someone's front yard or victory garden and was killed by cats, dogs, cars, or the gardeners themselves. What a wonder it is that any of these unprotected creatures live to grow up! The nest is often placed in the most conspicuous spot where the sun will warm it. It is a mere hollow in the ground about five inches deep and six or seven inches square, just about large enough for you to fit your two fists in it. It is grass-lined and downy with fur plucked from the mother's breast. Cottontail nests are so carefully covered with grass and leaves that there is no use in trying to find them. They are only discovered when the nest has been abandoned or laid bare by accident. While nursing her young, the mother's only real defense is her lack of odor so that there is no chance of her being tracked by the best hunting dogs. But for fear of being seen, she must leave her helpless, blind, and unfurred young alone throughout the day. To show herself would be to risk giving away the secret of the nest's location where there may be from four to eight or even thirteen young ones.

Sometimes her nest is discovered by well-meaning children who 'rescue' the babies and carry them home, thinking that they have been deserted or orphaned and not knowing that at dusk the anxious mother will steal out of her hiding-place near-by and creep under the loose cover of the nest to feed and wash her young ones, and then steal away to nibble at the green shoots of plants and shrubs. The mother cottontail is always close by, since her home-ground is but an acre or two. There she has four or five 'forms,' which is the name for the daytime resting-place of cottontails. If you know how to read the pressed-down weeds and grasses in field, hedge, and blackberry thicket, you can discover these forms that have sheltered the owner through rain, snow, wind, or hot summer days. Each is no doubt carefully chosen for certain weathers and dangers. And so in one of these forms sits the mother of the babies that seem so neglected and motherless. Only two or three times during the night does she return to nurse them.

After about ten days, when they are fully furred, their eyes begin to come open, and at the age of two or three weeks these tiny babies begin their adventures alone in a world of enemies. Cottontails seem born only to furnish food for hunters and the meat-eating birds, animals, and snakes.

When the cottontail babies are brought to Trailside, they are usually still blind. Sometimes their dark, sleek coats still bear the loving and neat tongue marks of their mother's last washing when she smoothed their fur and brushed it up across their blunt foreheads so few hours before. Never again are they to look so tidy and well-cared-for. At this stage they are altogether lovely with ears like furry new leaves not yet unfolded. As soon as the eyes come open, the ears begin to stand up, the fur fluffs out, and the babies totter about with little buglike hops.

For many days they huddle in a smooth, compact nest-shaped group, and I know few things nicer than to run my hand across their warm silkiness. Although most of them refuse food for a day or so, they do not become noticeably thinner or weaker. Warm milk from a medicine dropper is then taken readily, but I have been more successful in providing them with a small dish of milk or cream — rabbit milk is very rich in

butter fat — and letting them choose how much and when as soon as they can learn to drink. In this way there is far less danger of overfeeding. Water, of course, is always placed in the cage, along with raw oatmeal, crushed oats, delicate dandelion leaves, fresh grass and clover, lettuce if it is dry, and thinly sliced carrots and apples. Most of these, however, are merely substitutes for a natural diet — but who has the time and the sharp eyes to learn just what it is that baby rabbits nibble in the meadows at night!

Like all wild creatures the bunnies are happiest when in hiding and so they should have a heap of dry grass to creep under. When possible I use the so-called Spanish moss which grows on Southern trees. It is loose and warm and yet doesn't fall apart and can be used for weeks.

Baby cottontails are very shy and sometimes squeal shrilly when handled — leaping twelve inches straight up at every attempt to pick them up. I always place them on sawdust in a wire-mesh cage with no jagged edges or large spaces through which they might escape, for little rabbits have an amazing power of finding even a high-up opening and squirming through.

I regret to say that, in spite of my best efforts, there is a high death rate, and it seems best to release them as soon as they are able to eat and run. Although I have never succeeded in rearing them past five months, I have talked with visitors who have been luckier. Even a roomy outside cage on the ground seems not to satisfy their wants and death comes suddenly from unknown causes in the form of intestinal troubles or weakness in the hind quarters. It is said that this country has no wilder animal than the little cottontail who so often can be seen hopping tamely about back doors and gardens. So far as I know, none of the large zoos have been able to maintain a successful colony of them.

Among our visitors are two persons who owned exceptional cottontails. One pet, raised indoors with the family dog, lived to the age of ten years. The other was a wild one named Nancy, who, lured by some magic in a friendly voice and patient hand, would steal out at dusk from the garden shrubbery and, leaping upon the knees of the old gardener, would allow herself to be stroked. Her trust in him was so great that openly, in broad daylight, she visited her nest in the adjoining meadow.

The one shining star in our Trailside record is a cottontail cherished for its outlandish markings. He is named Blitzen, the German word for lightning, because his nose and part of his face is a snowy-white, unlike most cottontails, who usually bear a narrow brush stroke of white on the forehead. His eyes were not brown, but a brilliant blue! With five others, he grew up in an outside cage. It seemed that at last we were to succeed in rearing these delicate wild creatures in captivity. Then there was a tragic week or two in August when everyone watched and waited as the other five died, one by one. Every morning Blitzen was sitting in the hollow log. One week, two weeks, three weeks passed: at last he seemed safe, but I have always thought that Blitzen, the only one of the six who was nursed and weaned by his own mother, was, by this very fact, immune to the malady that destroyed the others. In the struggle against disease, the bottle-fed orphan has fewer chances than his luckier wild brothers.

School reopened in the fall and busy children found little time

71

to come to Trailside. When the nights grew frosty the lone little blue-eyed cottontail was brought indoors. It was then that I discovered that his right eye had turned to the dark brown of all normal cottontail eyes while the left remained that brilliant blue! During a few weeks the change had taken place, and no one had noticed how or when it had happened.

For a cottontail he was strangely tame, but he looked so forlorn and lonely that I began to wish that there could be a Dunder to keep him company. Where to find a black Dunder? Black is rare among animals, and though we had two skunks they were inseparable. There were, however, two young female black rats, the first ever born here to a white mother. One was picked and introduced to Blitzen with the hope that it would not follow its rat nature of slyly nipping at animals of another species. Dunder and Blitzen liked each other immediately. Dunder, being of a much more curious turn of mind, examined every inch of Blitzen, sniffed in his ears, roughed up his fur, and gently nibbled up and down his spine, a courtesy which seems to be a custom of greeting and identi-

DUNDER, THE RAT, AND BLITZEN, THE RABBIT

fication among rat people. They were the best of friends. When Blitzen, who often spent the night running free in the museum, was put back in his cage, Dunder pounced on him and in great excitement made her minute examinations all over again. They fed from the same dish, and on lazy days Blitzen sprawled full length and Dunder draped herself comfortably across his neck or back and together they slept by the hour. Sometimes at night Dunder tried to play and would perform a funny little dance all around Blitzen, nipping gently, but as rabbits don't play in this manner Dunder would be placed back in the rat cage every so often to have fun with her own kind. Fun to a rat seems to consist of tussling over a bone, mock fights and wrestling matches, sleeping in a heap four deep in a wire basket, and the careful grooming of each other's coats. Dunder was always welcomed home and never had to go through the bullying and cross-examinations that strange rats must submit to before they are accepted. Once the other black rat was accidentally placed in Blitzen's cage, but I soon discovered the mistake because there was no friendliness on the part of the rat, who nipped the rabbit at every chance.

Blitzen, too, has his nights and days of freedom. He and John, our big white rabbit who has never been locked up in a cage, have a peculiar kind of friendship. Their evenings begin with John cleaning the cottontail's coat, and the two then sit in quiet meditation with John resting his head on Blitzen's. But invariably they end up with Blitzen pulling large bunches of John's white coat right out of his skin. In the morning the museum floor is strewn with blobs of white fur, and I always have a moment of panic until I locate the two, safe and unhurt, after their night's escapade, both looking as if nothing unusual had happened.

Blitzen, so different from other cottontails in appearance, is also of a different temperament — for although no efforts were made to tame him in those first months, he turned out to be tame anyway. He seems to like to be petted and held and always gently licks arms or fingers once he is caught. However, while on the floor all of those wild instincts prompt him to escape capture. Unlike

73

even the smallest of bunnies, who can pinch unmercifully, he has never used his sharp teeth to nip anyone who holds him.

This mild friendship of Dunder and Blitzen is always a pleasing picture. The good will and understanding between an animal of one species and another of unlike species seems to be a sort of sign of that beneficence we seek in Nature. I have seen that sign at the moment when a young squirrel leaped onto the back of Bambi, our fawn, as he stepped delicately over the unfearing cottontails. I have seen it when Bambi walked casually across the room with a dove on his back or when he bobbed his head in friendly recognition to John, the rabbit, whenever the rabbit passed him. These were always breathless moments when it seemed as if a door were being partly opened and we were permitted to glimpse some secret of Nature in a mood close to the Nature in the landscape of the fables and poetry of childhood.

10. Salamanders

IN THE OLD DAYS, when the alchemists, who tried to turn the baser metals into gold by magic, believed Fire, Earth, Air, and Water were peopled with fairy creatures, they called the wild and beautiful beings dwelling in the heart of the flames salamanders.

The name came to be used in connection with all sorts of implements used by persons whose work dealt with fiery furnaces, whether they were bakers or smelters of iron. Country people in Europe today might tell you that a salamander is a poker with which to stir up the fire. Nowadays plasterers will tell you that it is a stove in which charcoal is burned in order to dry a newly plastered wall. The name was even applied to certain traveling show people who made their living by eating or walking through fire, so that the very recent fire-fighters in war-bombed London were also called salamanders.

It was through the belief in spirits living in flames that the sleek little creature who haunted the damp places of cellars and woodpiles, spring houses and stone-floored kitchens, came to be named a salamander, for how natural that, when a living creature darted through the fire on the hearth, people were only too willing to believe that they could live unharmed in the flames and were some form of fairy creature. Actually the poor animal was probably driven by the heat from the hollow log or the woodpile in which he had taken shelter for his long winter sleep — only to vanish as if by magic when he was burned to a crisp in the flames.

The salamander of this country is perhaps the least well known of all of the cold-blooded tribe of animals. He is to be found in water or in moist places, and then only at night or on rainy or cloudy days. In certain locations where they are locally abundant, he may be discovered making his spring migration to the ponds for breeding and egg-laying. If he has a slippery, wet skin, toes without claws, eyes without eyelids, and ears without openings, he is a salamander, and not the lizard that almost everyone calls him when they see him for the first time. In fact 'Spring Lizard' is the name by which he is known in many country districts.

The salamander is an amphibian — he can live both on land or in the water. The animal group known as amphibian includes frogs and toads. Most amphibians begin life as tadpoles or polliwogs which hatch from jellylike eggs that were laid in water. When their legs and arms develop, they are no longer gill-breathers, but crawl forth from the water as air-breathers to spend the rest of their lives in moist places under logs or stones or in the water.

Unlike the tadpoles of toads and frogs, the young salamander tads require living or moving food, in the form of tiny water creatures. This makes the rearing of any number of them quite a problem. Out of a great cluster of eggs which hatched in the museum, we succeeded in bringing one through the change. He was the sum total of all his unluckier brothers and sisters who ate each other and were finally eaten by him! I regret to add that the victor himself became a link in the food chain when he in turn was devoured by the bullfrog.

The hatching of this cannibalistic family of Spotted salamanders was a long and fascinating process. The clear globes of jelly with their dark germ of life could be held in the palm of one's hand, and as they rolled about like pellets of quicksilver, the half-inch wriggling tadpoles could be seen swimming within them as though eager to be free. When they were at last released from their crystal prisons at about the end of a month, the tadpoles spent some days clinging to the curtain of delicate green alga plants that festooned the tank. Their first nourishment was these. Then began the fight to the death. Each day the numbers diminished until only a few strange-looking little creatures like miniature sea monsters remained floating lazily in the tank, their plumy clusters of gills drifting off from either side of the neck. The survivor of all these little water beasts lost his gills in solitary splendor, and, unobserved for one day, he simply appeared as a full-fledged salamander three inches in length, his black body mottled with dull yellow.

Among the kinds of salamanders two nice ones to keep as pets are the Spotted and the Tiger, both of which live for many years and always feed eagerly. The food of the adult salamanders must also either be alive — worms, insects, snails — or raw meat offered on the end of a moving finger or stick. When a newly captured salamander dashes away from the food, try dangling before him a bit of raw beef on an unknotted string. Gently pull the string from the mouth as soon as he has clamped down on it.

If you feed him by placing the meat on the end of your finger, it will be rather exciting as his swift lurch and snapping jaws always come as a surprise, and very often you'll find your finger halfway down his throat. But as his teeth are only strong enough to grip the prey, you will not feel so much as a prick, although you may have some trouble convincing him that your finger is not edible.

When two salamanders stalk like hunters, nose to ground, a big night crawler and come to grips — as they both catch hold of an end of it — there is a slow tussle. First one and then the other is dragged and thrown this way and that, and it reminds one of their ancient ancestors who wallowed in the black ooze of the swampy, carboniferous world millions of years ago.

What battles those must have been when a couple of eight-foot salamanders both aimed and captured the same cockroach,

especially since in those days the cockroaches were two feet long!
Back and forth these monsters must have slapped their huge-
headed, fat bodies, sending down showers of golden spore dust as
they crushed the tree ferns and giant rushes that grew to twenty
feet in height along the edges of the steaming ponds and lakes.
Their battlegrounds added one more layer of decaying plant life
to the great coal beds that were to be born from this age.

Nowadays the longest Spotted or Tiger salamanders measure
only about seven inches in length, although occasionally they reach
ten inches. Only one small giant salamander is left on earth, a
five-foot salamander found in the mountain streams of China and
Japan.

Spotted salamanders have lived twenty-four years in captivity.
They are best kept in a tank of water where rocks and logs provide
a sloping rest partly out of water, where they enjoy spreading out.
Without water or extremely moist surroundings the salamander
cannot live, because, like all amphibians, instead of drinking water,
he absorbs it through his slime-covered skin which for that reason
must never be allowed to dry out.

11.

Mr.
Peewee,
The Screech Owl

IT WAS A WARM, DARK NIGHT, the last one in the month of May. Tall lush weeds had taken the place of the spring flowers that had swept through the leafless woods earlier. Violets, spring beauties, anemones, trilliums, wild geranium, adder's-tongue lilies — all were gone. Although we could not see them, we knew that only the white medallions of the mayapple were all that remained of the woodland flowers of spring.

The trail that Littlejohn and I were following was dark and velvety. Every bend promised some sudden adventure, but the still, warm air remained undisturbed by any such exciting sounds as

79

we had hoped for. Then it happened; a tiny complaint came out of the tangle of weeds beside the path. It was really useless to look. Surely it was only a mouse — but we rustled the weeds and listened. There it was again, a soft hiss. "Possum!" we said in one breath and got down on our knees. The hiss came again and from the very same place. 'Baby 'possum!' we whispered. Littlejohn struck a match, but in the dim, dying light of it, all we saw were the white blobs of mayapple blossoms. Other matches were lighted, and each time the pleading little complaint quavered up from the darkness. Then we saw it. What we had thought was just another mayapple blossom was a little round ball of white fluff. In the flicker of the last match we saw a downy little gnome with a worried look in its squinting eyes. We saw that we had an owlet, not an opossum.

All the way home we took turns holding it, because there is nothing so fascinating as the warmth and the peculiar heaviness of a small living creature resting in the palm of one's hand. We could feel the little round belly with its bare spot and the softly balancing feet still too young to grip. Back at Trailside we discovered him all over again under the light and identified him as a screech-owl baby! He weighed just two ounces. The pupils of his pale amber-rimmed eyes were still cloudy-blue. He was almost snow-white in his thick downy covering of baby fluff. His bluish beak was about as large as it was ever to be and so were his pale fluff-covered legs and feet. His tail was a ridiculous little fan.

Luckily we were well supplied with fat night crawlers which he accepted with eagerness, gobbling them down whole. We had quite a few shopworn robin nests which had served as nurseries for countless robins, starlings, and jays, but we felt little Mr. Peewee would be unhappy in that sort of nest. So we did our best to give him something to take the place of the hollow tree from which he had evidently fallen. This was a wooden parakeet box with a small round entrance hole and a removable top. Three inches of fine sawdust covered the floor of the box.

Here Mr. Peewee slept most of the time for the next few days. His droppings were always found in the corners of the box so that his feet and feathers never became soiled. We were careful not to keep our baby owl out of his nest box for more than five minutes at a time. Because, like all young things, he needed rest, darkness, and sleep during that period when he would still have been nesting under the downy breast of his mother, not yet ready to face the daylight except for a curious peek now and then. Perhaps it was this curiosity of his that had caused his fall from the nest hole we had discovered high up in the oak under which we had found him. He was certainly no orphan, because the head of an adult bird peered out for a moment as we stood wondering if that were the nest hole.

The first few days little Mr. Peewee didn't walk. He just sat on his heels wherever he was put. But he did a lot of stretching, and it was quite wonderful to watch him begin to grow an inch and a half taller during the process. He even stretched his feathery toes and made them curl up at the tips. One at a time he stretched his wings downward and showed the tiny brown quills that were developing at their tips, but when he folded them again they vanished into his downy coat and there was hardly a trace of wings at all.

Meanwhile his face acquired a soiled appearance with the

sprouting of the dingy pinfeathers that were to become a fine set of gray whiskers fanning downward and outward on each side of his nose.

Long before Mr. Peewee could climb through the little round window of his house, he discovered that it was a fine peekhole, and after his frequent naps he would stand on tiptoe and peer out with one bleary eye at the strange new world around him. Mr. Peewee was lovable and laughable, even though he only stood and stared, but he was all of that and more when he began to walk. Hunching over with neck thrust forward, he stalked along giving a queer impression of having his hands in his hip pockets.

Ten days after his arrival he began to clutch with his feet at any object he happened to step on. A tiny dead sparrow was given to him and he immediately showed himself to be the son of a hunter. He went through all the motions of a bird of prey with its kill, clutching and hovering over the sparrow and making realistic tearing motions with his beak and then bobbing his head up and down to make sure no enemy caught him off guard. It was all very authentic except that not a feather of the sparrow's body was disturbed, because Mr. Peewee accomplished only a few futile licks at it. But it was valuable practice. After he'd amused himself for a while, the bird was cut in pieces and fed to him complete, bones, feathers, entrails, all of which slipped down his gullet with surprising ease.

In spite of this grown-up act, Mr. Peewee was still not yet too clear-sighted. The pupils of his eyes were still clouded with the mists of babyhood. He was none too sure of his aim when food was presented some distance from his mouth. However, he had more than doubled in weight and tipped the letter scales at four and one-half ounces. As he spent much less time in sleeping, a change of house was necessary. Another larger parakeet box was used, and shortly afterward it was necessary to enlarge the entrance hole so that he could go in and out to sit on the perch in the small cage where his nest box had been placed. The day those alterations took place, he was so long without his familiar box that he grew tired of waiting for his nap and was discovered flat on his belly with his head in the corner where the box had stood. Somehow whenever I caught him lying down to sleep in this fashion, it seemed as strange as seeing a horse asleep on its side. All of our grown-up owls always sleep on a perch, so we never thought of him resting flat like other baby birds in a nest.

Peewee's meals were early and often, although he began to show a marked interest in food after dark as he grew older, and began to eat from a dish, his diet being as near natural as we could supply. Many fledgling birds and bunnies died, despite our efforts, so there was plenty of necessary natural food in his baby days when bones were forming. His appetite was amazing. We knew that he should have bones, feathers, fur, and entrails as well as muscle meat, but it was always wonderful to watch when he quietly downed all of this indigestible material. An owl's digestive system extracts all of the usable material. The roughage is rolled up into a tapered pellet and cast up from the stomach. Peewee dropped his first obligingly into the hand of a boy holding him. It contained bits of fur and feathers, bones apparently having been soft enough to digest.

On the seventeenth day after his arrival at Trailside, Mr. Peewee weighed five and one-half ounces and stood five and one-half inches high. Also, on that day, after considerable aiming and planning, he made his first flight. It wasn't much, only a yard or so to the top of a near-by cage. Of course, by this time he was well-feathered, but the down still attached to the tips of the quills and body feathers made him seem still very babyish.

For several days he practiced this flight, both up and down, and then began to look longingly toward the top of the more distant door. At this time he would sit on my desk in the evening owling everything in sight and especially his own moving reflection in the glass doors of the bookcase. An owl's hoot away in the woods, his young brothers and sisters were no doubt making their first practice flights to branches above the nest hole, but Mr. Peewee's education was very different. He was discovering the curious fascination of his own shadow at his feet. He would nibble at it, clutch the air with one clenched foot, pick up nothing, and carefully examine it. His movements would cause his leaf-size shadow to move and he would begin all over again in an effort to pick it up. When I made shadow pictures with my hands on the wall, Mr. Peewee's eyes widened and diminished as he followed every motion of shadow ducks and eared creatures. Down would go his head, and then round and round with his unmoving eyes staring straight ahead. Perhaps at this time Mr. Peewee was able to distinguish only movement and dark objects.

The twenty-second day was also an important day for Peewee and his human friends. He was given a young but fair-sized dead rat to play with. Had we not returned to his cage a few minutes later, just in time to see the tail of the rat disappear, we should have found it hard to believe it possible for him to have swallowed whole anything of this size. For one awful moment we felt that he had made a tragic mistake, but Peewee gulped again, and his tightly shut eyes came open with an unmistakable look of complacency. That afternoon, when the rat was well on the way to digestion, Mr. Peewee owled the door some twelve feet away, aimed carefully, and took off only to flatten out against it below the top and fall dazed to the floor. Twice he missed before he reached the top. From this day on he was a flyer.

On the fortieth day, Mr. Peewee, although still silvered with baby fluff above his coppery feathers, was free to fly anywhere in the museum both day and night. He was now in perfect control of his movements in the air and resented bitterly his confinement for the night. His nest box was placed on a high case in the mounted-bird room and there he retired several times during the hot days to sleep so soundly that no amount of knocking on its walls would wake him. Often when his prolonged absence became alarming, we had to climb up and peek in to make sure that he was there. Sometimes he wasn't there and would be found asleep in a box of rags in the basement. At night we safeguarded him from drowning by covering the deepest fish tank with a screen cover. Screech owls

84

are excellent fishers and Peewee showed a great interest in all of the tanks.

Although Peewee never learned to come at a call and would not fly down to our shoulders, he often arrived in the thick of things. There would be a cool breeze overhead and there, as if by magic, would be Peewee perched at eye-level returning stare for stare, as curious to see visitors as they were to see him.

He continued to be affectionate and playful and loved to be petted and scratched about the ears and mouth or to have his beak gently pulled or tapped. He would grasp our fingers in his needle-sharp claws and pretend to be eating, but he never dug in and held on with his claws as only a screech owl can when it wishes to. Placed on a shoulder, he would preen and comb one's hair, shut his eyes and look the picture of contentment.

One of Peewee's favorite perches was on the top of the kitchen cupboard. One day during a lot of water-running, he hopped down to a lower shelf and began to chitter. Obviously he wanted something. We lifted a cup of water up to him and he dipped his head in. Peewee was ready for his first bath. The signs were unmistakable. Someone ran for a large flat pan, and meanwhile we took away the small dish, but Peewee, being quite carried away by the idea, went right on going through the motions of taking a bath. By the time the new pan was filled and he had been placed in it, he was all out of the idea and so we left him. But after a short while he was ducking and splashing in his first real bath. He came out looking anything but like a well-groomed owl. Bathing continued daily and sometimes oftener throughout the warm weather, when it stopped with the first of the cool autumn days.

During his fifth month, Peewee began to surprise and delight everyone by alighting on shoulders and for the first time giving his soft eerie call. This, however, did not continue for very long, as he soon learned that well-meaning but inexperienced hands were likely to try to capture him.

One night I had just settled down to do some painting in the basement when Peewee landed on my shoulder in his usual un-

believable silence. In spite of the strong odor of paint and tur-
pentine, Peewee remained there peering down at the work, which
held his interest for some twenty minutes.

By the latter part of August, Mr. Peewee had completed his
first moult and had feathered out with beautiful coppery feathers
mottled with white. Sleek, trim, and amber-eyed, he took on a
truly owlish dignity and retired for the better part of the day to the
basement, where several dark corners high up served as a substitute
for his natural hollow-tree home. At other times he waited pa-
tiently for someone to open a dark closet on the main floor into
which he darted and stayed for hours at a time. His nursery box
was forsaken except at rare intervals when he seemed to enter it
only in a spirit of play in order to bob his head in and out and climb
back and forth through the hole.

During the day he spends many waking hours looking out of
the windows and registering his reactions by growing tall and thin
and raising his ear tufts at the sight of distant dogs or anything
moving on the streets. Sometimes he perches on the top sash and

soaks up the hot sunshine by dropping and spreading his wings. His curiosity is never satisfied. The evening feeding of young squirrels with milk in a medicine dropper brought him out of the dark rooms, and only the click of his claws on the desk warned me that he had entered the pool of light to frown his nightly disapproval that he could not get at these tiny fat wriggling creatures and make a meal of them. His expression at this time was sheer shocked disgust, and he watched for a while, standing stiff and alert and bent backward ever so little as if both fascinated and repelled.

Food is placed out for him in the evening, but in the forenoon, when the main meal for the museum animals is being prepared, Peewee often perches on the shelves of the food table and eagerly takes bits of raw cold meat with a chittered thanks resembling the delicate little acknowledgment that cats give when spoken to or offered a tidbit.

Just after Peewee's plumage had reached its finest, his curiosity led to a near tragedy. He was found hopelessly tangled in sticky flypaper. It was a week or two before his feathers were entirely cleaned by the aid of alcohol and benzine used sparingly. During that time, we realized the past beauty of Mr. Peewee's silent, velvety flight, for while the downy surface of his wings was glued flat, his flight was flappy and distinctly audible. Was it our imagination that fancied that he wore a hunted look until all was right?

Mr. Peewee is grown-up now and is greatly given over to nighttime activities. No doubt he catches a mouse or a moth occasionally. He is often seen carrying the egg case of a spider which he has dug from the dusty corners he haunts. When we walk through the dark museum rooms, he skims back and forth and so frequently does he sideswipe one's shoulder or head that we are convinced it is sheer mischief or perhaps an irresistible desire to aim and touch a moving object, just to keep his 'hand in.'

Since his eighth month he has had spells of being very antisocial, and instead of merely dipping and fanning, he plunges down on the heads of strangers and digs in his claws in no gentle manner. This has earned him the nickname of Mr. Peewee 38, after the pursuit plane known as P38, as well as solitary confinement in a basement cage occasionally. Some persons seem to arouse his enmity more than others, and Littlejohn and I have been proud to note that, being his very closest friends, he never mistakes us for someone else in the dark. Whether this unpleasant trait is to be part of his nature or whether it is merely a passing phase of his maturity we do not know.

There is no doubt that should Mr. Peewee go winging forth into the wide night through some carelessly unclosed door he will be well able to fend for himself. As the Mock Turtle in *Alice in Wonderland* practiced reeling and writhing, so Mr. Peewee has had long practice in dipping and diving, in skimming between furnace pipes and ceiling, in leaping away from swiftly closing doors, in plummeting down the spiral stairwell and the steep basement stairs, and in zigzagging through the museum rooms. Released from the hand, he can bank and turn like lightning at a perfect right angle. His daytime antics and his haunting presence after dark have given us one more secret glimpse of one of the creatures of the night and how they grow from babyhood to wild and lovely maturity.

12.

Fox and Gray Squirrels

THERE ARE SOME ANIMALS that we love for their beauty —others, such as toads and English bulldogs, for their ugliness; some because they are tame or because they never will be tame. That's the nice thing about being an animal-lover; you like them all and for different reasons. Of course, everyone has favorites about which he'd rather talk than any other. Mine are squirrels, and I suppose this is because some fifty of them have taken up a great deal of my time and thoughts, plans and hopes. There were tiny babies who died in my hand. There were big ferocious fellows who stayed long enough to heal a lame leg and were released, still chattering as angrily as they did the day they arrived. One hand-raised pet, paralyzed in her hind legs for a year, was the most 'human' of them all.

Every spring and fall the squirrel babies arrive at Trailside. Some plainly show that their mothers have tried desperately to

89

carry them to a new den or back to the one from which they fell. The mother's little tooth marks on belly and chest show how she hurried and how her teeth closed on skin too thin to hold as she sprang out of harm's reach, forced to leave them and to watch them carried away by the first passer-by. And so any fall or spring day a box is brought to Trailside by that passer-by, and under the old sweater at the bottom of it there is a fat little fox squirrel or perhaps a baby gray squirrel that is all legs and resembles a hairy reptile.

Now, tiny fox squirrels with eyes still sealed are the most truly beautiful and appealing babies that I know. They combine the universal appeal of the very young with that very new miniature creation of delicate perfection. Every line and attitude of their slumbering bodies is a delight to examine. Many minutes can be spent gazing at the perfection of each sleek fold of skin, each shade of coloration, the direction of the hair growth, still smooth and satiny, and the creamy petal-like texture of the bareskinned belly with its faint, white patch where milk shows through.

Soon the squirrelet learns that the human hand is warmth, food, and pleasure, and when its eyes come open at the age of twenty-eight days, it seeks the hands and the shoulders of a human as it would the protection of its mother or the den tree. It knows no other world and, moreover, it has lost its mother before it was possible for her to instill in it those lessons of fear, caution, and flight. A few little warning signals from her during danger-haunted nights and days in the wild and the lesson would have been learned, never to be unlearned by any human coaxing. But there is growth and adventure and a new kind of wisdom for him in the human world. As we watch the little squirrel and try to know what is best for his happiness and health, we soon discover that young as he is he has a personality of his own and also that he will show us many secret things about all squirrels.

Knowing squirrels is much more than recognizing them. Knowing them means to know how they yawn, how they stretch, when they are having fun, where they like to be scratched, what they like best to eat, how their eyes look when they mean trouble, what their anger cry is. It means knowing what is meant by the tiniest gesture, what sounds will make them dash to safety, what sounds will make them playful, sleepy, or contented — all of these things and dozens more you must discover before you can really know squirrels, or any other animal for that matter.

That's why squirrels are such fun. You are always looking for some new mood or feeling and very often finding it. It's like playing a game to sit and watch three or four young squirrels in their cage. Your mind races ahead of them, knowing so many times exactly what they are going to do next and why. Sometimes you have only to hear them to know what they are doing.

Out in the woods it is a rare thing to be able to get close enough to squirrels to see them in their gentler moods when they are playing and acting 'squirrely.' Who ever saw a wild squirrel fall asleep or wake up? Who ever found one asleep? All of those things which go on in the dark warm little nests are secret. It is only when you have three or four young squirrels being raised together that you see charming little snatches of animal play and affection. Usually light sleepers, even at night, they waken at the slightest sound and lie there, wide-eyed, waiting to find out if it's safe to move, and then they begin to wiggle down into warmer and more cozy places. There is much arranging and rearranging of legs and arms, loose corners of the flannel or sweater, which is their bed, are pulled and tucked. Then they begin to play, gently as kittens. One lies flat on its back with outspread curled paws, one sits up and, taking the other's paw in both of hers, begins to wash or gently to nibble it up and down from fingertips to elbow. Ears, too, are carefully gone over, and how the drowsy one enjoys it! Her teeth chatter and she moves her head comfortably, and all of a sudden she is sitting up nibbling the face and ears or tail of the other one who is now stretched out. Gradually they become drowsy and soon all are asleep. The companionship and devotion they share with each other during the day is expressed in their affectionate sleeping embrace. So long as they share their cage and nest this affection and efficient grooming and cleaning of each other's coats will go on between them. In the daytime, of course, the play is often swift and kitten-like. Over and over they roll without a sound even on the hard wood floor. Leaps and tackles end a wild chase. Friendly nips sometimes bring forth a squalling complaint that says as plain as day, 'Ouch, you pinch too hard!' or 'Don't, I tell you, that hurts!'

The language of animals is an old, old question. If talking is being able to make you understand what they mean, then young squirrels surely are the greatest of all talkers. They talk out loud and use, I'm afraid, very bad language at times. But they also know how to whisper and speak softly, and they have a wonderful and complete sign language.

Everyone who has watched squirrels in the woods or parks knows a little about their angry words and their alarm signals, those coughing, sputtering barking words punctuated with tail signals. Their fine, plumy, graceful tails wig-wag and flick up and down and round and round into question marks and exclamation points, as the squirrel expresses his opinion on all things, those which concern him as well as those which do not concern him. Squirrels, like bluejays, carry all the news of the forest but if you are to hear all of their large vocabulary you must learn some of it from a squirrel who lives indoors.

FOX AND GRAY SQUIRRELS

The first cry of the baby squirrel even before its eyes are open is that of hunger and distress or pain. It is one of the most piercing of animal sounds. When I first heard it I recognized it instantly as a cry for help. It seemed to come from everywhere in the museum, but of all my Trailside pets none had ever made a sound like that. Several minutes passed before I discovered that a two-ounce mite of a squirrel had crawled out of its blanket, and clinging to the wire bars of its cage with a stricken look on its face, was giving forth this whistling shriek that meant hunger and the need for the comforting attentions required by animal babies as well as by human babies. This cry must be heard by a mother squirrel when she is at least a block distant from the nest. I've seen one of my four-months-old squirrels stand its ground and use it effectively to rout an older squirrel determined to steal its food. The thief was only too glad to escape as far as possible from the deafening alarm signal.

The most interesting of squirrel talk is so small a sound as often to pass unnoticed. Both the old and young use it among themselves and to their human friends. Each time you go near their cage, or meet them, as you often do at eye level on some high place, they will greet you with soft little 'asking' sounds — little putt-putting grunts. It is a low, eager questioning. Sometimes it is the invitation to play when two squirrels meet on the museum floor. Squirrels and woodchucks are about the only small local mammals that show by sound as well as by action their friendly recognition of humans.

When you never miss a day in the life of a squirrel pet you are certain to have the fun of witnessing the first time he finds his voice — those barks and threats he will use toward enemies and unseen danger when he can truly fight his way. Serious as it is for the young squirrel it is most laughable to see. Out of the blue one day comes the urge and like a little bantam rooster he perches on a high place and begins to crow and wigwag his tail. He always appears to be as amazed as you are about what is happening to him and works himself up into a fine state. His call improves as he repeats it and then he begins slowly to turn in all directions broadcasting to the world his new-found power and confidence. At these moments I think he would face a lion, but suddenly the piercing look fades from his eyes and he is through. Once again he is the little handful of warm fur with feet and tail still too large for his body. Months may pass before the spirit moves him to crow again, but if you can find the right key sound you can often arouse him to reply vigorously.

Grays and fox squirrels, so different in ways and temperament, have many cries of anger and threat that are difficult to describe, and usually impossible to imitate. Gray squirrels have a long-drawn-out cry that seems to indicate unbearable mental misery. It is a complaint and a wail such as one would like to use during a bad toothache. It carries a long way through the woods, and once you have heard and identified it you'll never mistake it for any other cry. Ernest Thompson Seton describes it as a 'Qua, qua, qua, qua, qua-a-a.' Both males and females use it. Our grays in the museum sometimes have wailing days when even petting doesn't help them. The cry doubtless has a deeper meaning than mere annoyance, but it also indicates great displeasure. Sometimes it is accompanied by violent tail flicks, but usually the unhappy animal spreads out comfortably on a branch or your shoulder, stares straight ahead and begins to enjoy a long wailing period. Bobby, a sweet and gentle old female gray who lived over ten years, had a very definite sense of personal belongings. When her cage was washed and rearranged or repaired she spent the rest of the day wailing like a crotchety little old woman who had been disturbed at her fireside. I have never observed fox squirrels displaying this same kind of sensitiveness nor do they have a similar cry.

There was one instance when I believe that a squirrel was waiting to tell me what had happened. Puddin', a fox squirrel, whose tail and hind legs were paralyzed, had adopted and mothered a tiny three-months-old squirrel when it was placed in her cage. She was only a year old herself but she was devoted to the baby, and Lammie, as we called it, naturally clung to her because she spent most of her time lying quietly, and was for that reason a better substitute for a mother than the other three active squirrels in the cage. One day Lammie had a convulsion. After it was over there seemed to be no ill effects. A couple of days later when I came downstairs in the morning, I went straight to Puddin's cage as I always did. When I opened the door, Puddin', who was curled up in a heap of bedding outside of the nest box, literally flew out of the cage at me and clambered tooth and nail up to my shoulder, spluttering and talking as only she could. Her excitement lasted only a few minutes then I discovered Lammie's still little body lying among the bedding where Puddin' had been sleeping. I knew then that Puddin' had slept outside on the cage floor with the dead baby, and that when she was wakened by my arrival, her first instinct was to fly to me as she always did when some danger threatened or when anything happened that she could not understand. Lammie doubtless died in another convulsion, crying, as squirrels do, shrilly in pain and fear. Puddin', the sensitive little cripple, had not ignored Lammie's death as I have seen other squirrels ignore the deaths of their companions.

Good humor in a squirrel at any age is something spontaneous and unpredictable. Surely no animal delight can equal it. It has nothing to do with the high spirits of madly racing fawns or horses. There is no challenge in it, no fire. It is simple, gentle, delicate, and full of a sense of sheer nonsense and make-believe. They all have it, the grays, the foxes, the red squirrels, the old, the young, and even the crippled.

Puddin', in spite of her useless hind legs, could amuse herself by the hour with a dangling bit of cord tied from the roof of her cage, or by lying on her back and juggling a twig in her deft forepaws. She would hurl herself about the cage with lightning speed when the gleeful spirit moved her. When she was in a playful mood a bit of old soft quilt was placed in her cage and a branch stretched tightly from one end of the cage to the other just low enough for her to reach it. In an ecstasy of delight she would roll and tumble beneath it with closed eyes, open mouth, and kittenlike movements of her paws. She was acting silly and she knew it. With urging she would renew her clowning. Another cripple who could do everything but leap or sit up had the gayest of times throwing himself across the floor and rolling for sheer delight, or tackling his companions in football style.

I have found it not too easy and often impossible to coax Buttons, the tamest squirrel, to play anywhere except under the table where she has always played. Certain words spoken in a very high pitch and the sound of my fingers tapping rapidly on the floor usually cause her to clown. She jumps about stiff-legged with her back humped up, head down and eyes closed like a bucking bronco. At her maddest she has often run smack into a table leg which knocks the play out of her for awhile. She will stand up and box, and kick with all four legs while momentarily on her back. She delights to gnaw and tug at my fingers, skip off in small circles, pretend to bite, pretend to be chased, but observers or sudden sounds quickly stop the play. Buttons, who always arranges her bedding so that she can sleep on her back, loves to play at night and will waken at any hour to roll and tumble over and under my hand, never moving from the little hollow nest she has fashioned by heaping up her bedding of woolen rags.

Patty Cake, a young gray, was the greatest player of any squirrel I have known, though several other grays have shown all of the promise that I had time to develop in Patty. Once Patty found that a trick was fun, and worked, she repeated it until she was exhausted. Like all grays she was hard to stop once she started and no unusual sight or sound could interfere with her pleasure. The grays seem less delicate in their play, delighting in leaps that are often rash and unsuccessful, and in somersaults, and preferring to wind up the fun by getting too rough with teeth and claws in a general rough-house. As youngsters I have found them to be lighter and more agile than the chubby, stolid young foxes, although, oddly enough, the grays seem to mature more quickly while the foxes remain babyish for a year and a half. Patty once broke up a game of cards that was being played on the floor by leaping in and scattering the deck. That was fun, so she did it again. It became a regular performance when I took her upstairs with me in the evening. All she needed to go wild was to see and hear the red cards being snapped down on the floor and she would race between the players scattering the slippery cards like a miniature whirlwind. She was a born actor, too. Without protest she allowed herself to be dressed up in handkerchiefs, tied peasant fashion over her head. To be picked up by the head and forepaws was a signal for her to relax and play dead, letting her body swing and dangle lifelessly. Even when gently dragged along a table top she never moved a muscle until she sensed that the trick was over. Why she did it I don't know. Perhaps it is because grays, mad as they are, have the gift of relaxing. It may be that they are so soothed by pressure about the jaws that when experiencing it they would rather not move no matter what is done with them.

I have no intention of making it seem that Patty or any other squirrel is taught a trick in the same way in which a dog is taught. Squirrels have so many tricks of their own that all that is necessary is to begin handling them before they are weaned. This simply means before fear, caution, and mistrust are instilled in them by the mother's care. At that early age you have only to develop their personalities, which vary so greatly among individuals, and to guide their ways by association and by the repetition of sound and action. In my experience I have found the fox squirrel much less pliable in handling than the gray squirrel. I doubt if they could ever be trained to relax and expose their stomachs in the way that a gray will, just as I am sure that a skunk couldn't be taught to sit up and eat like a squirrel. It's not his nature. Whatever one does with these small, wild creatures must be done with the material they have to offer.

Oddly enough, although grays can relax so perfectly, they are great runners and race for the sheer love of it. As they pass a door or table leg they kick up and push off with both wiry hind legs in the most skittish and impertinent way imaginable. And yet both Patty and other grays I have known permitted their mouths to be opened so that any visitor could peer in and see the tiny molars way at the back of the jaws. When confined to her cage more closely during the busy summer months, Patty invented a game. Her toys were a whole nut and a half shell. Not always the same ones but any two that she found handy. She lay flat on her belly with the two nuts between her paws. Picking up one with her mouth she tossed it an inch or two to the side and then reached out and raked it back with the same paw while she picked up the other nut in her mouth and tossed it to the side. This was repeated for fifteen minutes at a time. You could always tell when Patty was playing by the two different sounds heard as the nuts tapped the tin floor of the cage.

Part of the charm of squirrels is, I suppose, the fact that they are never completely tamed. They give you the sense of being especially honored when they fall in with what you wish, and behave or perform as you wish them to. But the wild is never far from them even though they all learn their names so quickly. At any unpredictable moment your pet squirrel is likely to take to the higher places and sit staring, deaf to your sweetest coaxing tones and indifferent to tempting nuts. Sometimes it may become enraged or frightened for no apparent reason. Sometimes it becomes intent on stealing rags and papers in order to build a nest in some dark corner, even though it may never have been outside since its eyes were opened. Each one, however, is an individual with likes and dislikes and a personality of its own.

Many hand-raised squirrels never trust the human hand. There was Topsy, a fox squirrel, who would not tolerate handling, although she minded best of any when the frantic hour arrived to round up three to five galloping squirrels who raced at large throughout the museum before the doors were opened. It was always Topsy who obediently went to her cage first and hopped in when told to do so.

To me it is a never-ending thrill to call out a name over and over, wait, call again; finally to give up, and then to hear the patter and scud of hurrying feet on the basement stairs as Toby or Buttons comes skidding to me, breathless, with an air of having come as quickly as circumstances would permit, for they are always busy with burying a nut or finding where someone else hid one. I try to picture them listening, recognizing that that particular call is associated with them and me and frantically putting the finishing touches on whatever destruction or project they are engaged on. Even after a long wait their arrival, which always ends up with a flourish of speed, is always a reward, whereas the tardy arrival of Wendy, the dog, or Vickie, the cat, somehow seems only exasperating.

The welfare of a squirrel is dependent upon two important things — his plumy tail and his ability to stick to the tried and tested home ground. Besides being ornamental the tail serves many purposes. Without a long and well-feathered tail a squirrel would be unable to balance on the dizzy heights to which he climbs. Watch him walk a suspended cable, a narrow branch or roof gutter. Up and down goes the tail, shifting as his weight shifts, in exactly the same manner that a tight-rope walker in the circus shifts his long pole for balance. In an accidental fall or in the short, ordinary leaps the tail acts as a parachute, breaking the descent — although it might be many feet over the side of a precipice — and achieving a happy landing. It is said that a squirrel with a damaged tail rarely survives for long.

Besides all of these necessary uses the tail serves further purposes. It is a shield in bad weather, an airy, warm blanket under which its owner can curl up and sleep, a sunshade while he rests in the hot sun. Doubtless many a hawk has come away with half a squirrel tail while the owner fled to safety with his life.

Young squirrels make much use of their tail before they reach six months of age, seemingly spending much time learning its intricate uses. Since almost everything is strange and threatening to them, they approach all that stands in their path with a caution that is equaled only by their overwhelming curiosity, so that at times it is as if their approach were made up of two steps forward and one backward. The body is stretched out to its greatest

length, the hind legs far apart, and the tail, with all of its hairs rigidly on end, is swung out to the side and turned sidewise as a shield. With a sidling, gingerly motion they advance, caution and bravery eloquent in every move. You can all but see the sensitive hairs at the tail's end picking up the invisible message like delicate antennae.

This perfect control and co-ordination of tail and body is one of the most beautiful among animals. It is at the same time one of the most amusing of all animal poses. A little yellow-bellied fox squirrel seen from the rear as he sneaks up on a bit of waste paper looks for all the world like a funny little squatty bowlegged Indian in yellow buckskin breeches.

Tails come in for much grooming and combing. Three licks and a promise to head and ears never fails to wind up with a grand swipe with both paws in which the tail is gathered up and brought to the front and rapidly run over the face from its root to its tip. Whether this is a general checkup, or whether the tail, as some believe, is used as a towel, I have never quite decided. Whatever its meaning, young squirrels are forever doing it and even adults make this three-second grooming gesture at the least provocation. In the midst of a breathless chase they will take time out to hang by the toenails of the hind feet and swiftly rub the face with both forepaws before leaping to safety. It occurs so often when the squirrel is beset with excitement that I have come to think of it as an almost involuntary gesture similar to that of a man readying himself for what may come — you know, the hitch to the trousers and an added turn to the shirt sleeves.

Their face-washing, by the way, is a rather strange affair. It is never done with the same slow thoroughness with which a cat washes. Of course, the cat is a hunter and it is her business to be as odorless as possible in order to stalk such keen-scented animals as rats and mice. But like the cat, the gray and the fox squirrel are singularly devoid of personal odor so far as the human nose can detect. Theirs is merely the smell of dry fur. Although squirrels carefully groom each other's skin with sharp nibbling teeth, the

fur of face and head and paws is washed with lightning speed. Both paws are whipped over the back of the head and drawn down the nose or scrubbed round and round across the closed eyes.

The sniffy sound they make while doing it is actually made with the nose which provides the moisture rather than the mouth which is dry in order to facilitate spitting forth the hulls and skins of food. Squirrels are accurate and habitual spitters while eating, as they never eat the skin of even a berry. It is so much a part of their nature to peel their food that frequently they will peel a bit of already peeled banana. Of course the construction of the teeth and lips is such that spitting is quite easy.

102

FOX AND GRAY SQUIRRELS

The front teeth of the squirrel are long, chisel-edged incisors. There are two above and two below. Between them and the chewing teeth at the back of the jaws is a wide space where there are no teeth at all. With the front teeth he peels fruit and chips off the hulls of seeds and nuts or gnaws the nutshell to a fine powder. As he opens his jaws to do this, the lips fold inward and form a dry furry curtain behind the front teeth that all but closes the opening to his mouth. Food particles find no moist lips on which to stick. Nothing unwanted gets down his throat by mistake. With a tongue which is also very dry he flips or spits to right and left all that he does not wish to eat. Some squirrels will let you open their jaws but you cannot look down their throats without first holding aside the incurved lips that form the little curtain.

A second important faculty of squirrels is memory. It is memory rather than speed perhaps which saves the life of the squirrel most often. To escape he must know the way, for all the speed he can muster will not save him if he does not know where to run and how to dodge. Once learned it becomes second nature. Hundreds of times I have watched Lady, a wild squirrel, coming through the treetops to feed on the barn roof, and, long before she was close enough to recognize, I knew it was she by the route she traveled. A sure undeviating path through the branches of certain trees. Up and down and across, leaping here and dropping down there. She knows all of the blind alleys and dead ends and all of the clever escapes. She is on sure, home ground and so long as she stays in these two acres as she has for the past four years she will be safe. Let her get chased outside of her own bailiwick and she will lose much of her superb self-confidence and doubtless her very life.

Indoors our young museum squirrels are following the same wild instinct. As they learn a leap or an avenue of escape they practice it over and over again in a sort of mad frenzy, repeating the small pattern until you wonder that their unadventurous souls are content with the same silly routine. As wild squirrels have their particular trees where they know the way, the indoor squirrels who grew up in the museum have their particular play places. Sometimes it's such a favorite that you are always sure to find them there when they are not in their cages. They have their special fish tanks for drinking, their special curtain cords, resting places, and mischiefs. These spots are never forgotten. Sometimes an indoor squirrel may spend six months in an outside cage. As soon as it is released again in the museum it begins where it left off and goes unswervingly to its favorite haunts.

My contact with wild squirrels has been very meager, but I believe that I could wait and watch for many a year before I found an experience equal to one in which I was the villain and the heroine was a little mother squirrel, who had something which surpassed memory. An aquaintance of mine was troubled with fox squirrels in the attic of her home. To prevent their being poisoned, I agreed to trap them in a box trap and release them in the woods. Two yearlings were taken and on another day a bob-tailed mother squirrel. As I released the frantic old squirrel, I was greatly upset to see that she showed every sign of having recently nursed young ones, that were obviously back in the attic den.

Not twenty minutes later as I sat in an upstairs window of the museum, I saw a squirrel come down the path from the woods. Something in her attitude singled her out as a stranger and not one of the several strollers who come for handouts about six in the evening. Through the bird glasses I discovered that this was the bobtail just released a block away in the woods. I ran downstairs and out to the edge of the woods and saw her already far ahead of me bounding straight down the path. When I caught up to her she went up a tree and squatting on a low branch looked at me as I have never been looked at by any other squirrel. The rodent is not given to looking you in the eye and most pursued squirrels stay on the far side of the tree. This squirrel was different. Her whole bearing was one of calm determination and purpose. I think that it was not fancy that read into her eyes the fact that she recognized me as the evil doer and that she was bent upon not allowing any more interference. There was no mistake, her stubby tail and the bruise on her nose from fighting the trap were plainly visible as she sat a few feet above my head.

It was growing dark and chilly. I thought of the motherless babies alone in the attic and went sadly back home berating myself for having allowed this tragedy to happen. The next morning I called the uncordial owner of the attic to ask her to watch out for the mother squirrel. The hair rose on the back of my neck when I heard her say, 'Oh, she came back about seven this morning and the last we saw she and her two youngsters were crossing the carline and heading north.'

How did that squirrel find her way back to her babies over an unknown route, south through two blocks of woods and east for thirteen blocks through business and residence districts along a busy street with a carline on it? How did she do it with but an hour and a half of daylight between six in the evening and seven the next morning? Where did she spend the night? Not in the attic, for she was seen as she first entered the front yard on her return. And where at last did she go with her homeless babies that were still unweaned and could just walk without tottering? By the speedometer of my car her trip home measured one and two-tenths of a mile.

Friendship among female squirrels raised together is, I believe, for life if they are not separated. But they are solitary creatures in the wild and the separation of a pair of cage-mates over nine months of age seems to bring forth those dormant instincts of mistrust, making it impossible for either to tolerate the presence of the other again. I once separated a fox squirrel from the two grays that had been reared with it and in spite of two years of affectionate companionship between these three females, the grays turned on the fox squirrel after but a week's separation and not any scheme we devised could make them accept her again in their cage, or any other cage for that matter. The same has held true of female squirrels of the same species. Infant squirrels may often be introduced to a cage of females less than a year of age but never to older squirrels. The worst enemies, however, may be held at the same time and close together and, so long as one's hands are on them, they seem to enjoy the contact; but panic breaks loose the second they find themselves free of your hand.

Squirrels that are friendly quarrel among themselves as do all families and friends. They disagree and argue, particularly about food, the one being picked on doing all of the squealing and protesting. This does not prevent her from going right on with her peeling and gnawing. The thief has a peculiar and unvaried manner of attack. Up comes the greedy one and, standing beside the eater, places an arm about her neck and shoulder and with the other hand and her mouth tries to steal the tidbit. Often a quick paw is reached out to push or slap the thief. The argument goes on until one or the other finishes the food, but no bites are exchanged. It seems that biting is used only among true enemies and then as a last resort.

The forepaws which are used rapidly and both together are a common means of defense. A squirrel guarding some buried treasure in a common nest box will gnash her teeth and shake with rage when another passes the entrance. Efforts to enter are met with the usually effective gesture of slashing at the intruder with those short front arms. As the paws are armed with sharp curved claws that are capable of making several painful gashes in the skin of one's hand, no squirrel is careless enough to receive their slashes on its nose and face. Many other rodents such as mice, rats, woodchucks, muskrats, prairie dogs, chipmunks, and ground squirrels attack and defend in this manner. The rapidity of the motion can be gauged by the sound of the paws striking the cage wire when quarrels take place between caged and uncaged animals. The sound is like a stick snapped across cage bars.

Speaking of ill temper and anger, one amazing trait occurs when two caged squirrels are confronted with an enemy, such as a passing dog or some carnivorous animal whose whiff they get. They immediately turn on each other and for a few seconds there is a whirlwind fight. It is as if the odor of the enemy blots out every other familiar scent and they are momentarily blind with anger.

FOX AND GRAY SQUIRRELS

As for tolerating other creatures in the cage, no doubt many different kinds might be accepted by squirrels if they were placed together while still young. I have four yearling squirrels who have been reared with a white rat. Although there is no play between them they admit Cotton to their bed and carefully groom her whenever they run across her napping in a corner of their cage. A young skunk occasionally spent an afternoon in their cage. There was no resentment on either side and when the skunk curled up for a nap, each and every squirrel walked on him whenever they found him in their paths. Another pair of squirrels have shared a cage with three prairie dogs for many months. One of the squirrels grooms the dogs many times a day, and the dogs are often seen to come and sit waiting close by in the hope of the back rub or scalp treatment so efficiently given by this busiest of squirrels.

The successful arrangement of mixed families of animals is always interesting and often amusing, but the squirrels have a many-sided personality and show it at its best with their own kind. As one of a tame and congenial hand-raised group they will reveal gentle and endearing qualities in their life together and in their relationship with people.

There may be some who read this who have never seen the squirrel as anything but a burglar of attics and unused houses, a destroyer of green pear crops and a stealer of bird eggs. What human child and how many grownups have never done the same or worse? The eggs of the songbird as well as her fledglings are a legal prey in nature when a hungry squirrel's cravings lead him to the protein and calcium in the egg. The bird lays other eggs or chooses her nesting site more carefully and feeds her young the larvae of the tender insect songsters of the night, such as crickets, meadow grasshoppers, and katydids, as well as upon the beautiful and often rare butterflies. Far from condemning her we watch with delight as she crams the wriggling victim down her nestling's throat. You overlook much of Nature's message when you judge the wild killer and destroyer of nests in terms of human ideas of right and wrong. You miss all of the fascinating story of the interdependence between wild creatures when you do not see the taking of life as a part of Nature's scheme. Befriend and feed and study to know all of them, for even they are not always at war. The songbird has no unworthy foe except man, nor has the squirrel, although he is pursued by cat and hawk and a host of other animals.

13. Tarzan, The Raccoon

TRAILSIDE'S OLDEST PET is Tarzan, a raccoon, and in spite of his gentle, wistful face that has only the faintest trace of coonish mischief, he has managed to crowd a considerable amount of color and adventure into his eight years of museum life. One of my first chores when I came to Trailside was to remove the ancient adhesive tape from a forefoot which had been broken when he leaped from someone's arms into the drive and was hit by a car. By attracting his attention with acorns I contrived each day to cut a fragment free until the thick layers were all removed. This sounds simple enough but in my inexperience it was the most exciting moment of the day. Doubtless even at that time Tarzan would have submitted meekly to having the bandage removed all in one try but when you do a new thing with an animal new to you, you are wise to proceed slowly.

At that time Tarzan was a bachelor again after the death of his mate. The first autumn of my work at Trailside I was able to get him a new mate. She was no beauty, nine months old, yellowish, lean, and picked at random by the zoo keeper. Tarzan was all for being friends, but Jane was panic-stricken and for ten days nothing would tempt her to eat. One day a bit of buttered brown bread, accidentally dropped by a youngster assisting me in the cage, caused her to snatch greedily and devour it. Needless to say, she was given the rest of it while someone ran for all of the choice dainties the animal pantry could offer. The hunger strike was over. Jane ate with a huge appetite while Tarzan looked on with curiosity.

For weeks, though, she refused to so much as speak to Tarzan and spent her days huddled at the bottom of an upright hollow log. After teasing and coaxing for hours, Tarzan would come up and, standing on his new wife, would lean out of the small opening of the log looking bored and thoughtful. The log was sealed at each end and Tarzan's fat body completely blocked the entrance. The weather was unbearably hot, and being overly anxious about what an animal, without protest, would put up with, I would rescue poor Jane from what I was sure was slow death from heat exhaustion. Placing the log on its side was of little help as the same procedure followed. After wearing himself out in an effort to see at least her face, Tarzan would block the entrance and take the air in resigned comfort. When the log was removed from the cage Jane sought shelter, not in the roomy den box, but by wedging herself down in back of the half drum that served as their water tank. Tarzan would tease and pick and poke at her and then take his bath and purposely, I believe, tip the tank so far on its side that again it seemed necessary to rescue the child-bride. Never was such a honeymoon, but fortunately cold weather came and Jane was forced to respond to the need for animal warmth and Tarzan's fat bulk was the only refuge. Thus I found them one frosty morning locked in each other's arms in that quaint 'babes of the woods' fashion that coons have of sleeping in a half-upright position face to face.

But Jane never seemed a really good wife. There was little quarreling but neither was there any marked devotion between them. Like Jack Sprat and his wife they had different appetites. When fed, Tarzan grabbed for the meat and Jane was greedy for the fruit.

The next spring Tarzan was loaned to a scout camp for a weekend and managed to escape under the several large barracks buildings. Five days passed before I was able to locate two hunters with well-trained coon dogs, and though I hated the risk of having Tarzan killed by them, it was the only chance of our getting him back at all.

Late that night we drove out to the deserted camp in the woods and released the two dogs. It wasn't long before the owner recognized that particular kind of baying that the older dog used when he was in pursuit of a coon and not just following a trail. Knowing that Tarzan was out in the woods running for his life was one of my worst moments. The dogs were circling in from a field and the night was filled with their cries. Suddenly they stopped and we tore around to the other side of the huge building. Tarzan, instead of treeing, had gone under one of the buildings where he had doubtless been seeking shelter these past four nights. The dogs had followed. We all stood helpless listening to the growls and yelps of the dogs as Tarzan fought them off. At the point that seemed nearest to the battle preliminaries there was but one small hole in the hard, clay ground. At first the hunter could get only his head under the building. Before the dogs closed in, however, with only a second left before the real battle was to begin, the hunter managed to claw his way through the opening and grab Tarzan by the tail. We all pulled and the hunter came out holding the tail of something that sounded more like a wildcat than anything else. We were sure it was our coon because he has a very short tail compared to other coons. By flashlight the hunter had been able to distinguish Tarzan in the narrow low passageway formed by the side of the building and the floor joists. Creeping on its belly one dog was attacking Tarzan from the rear and forcing him straight into the path of the other dog facing him and only a few feet away. Through amazing luck Tarzan had arrived at the only spot where he could be rescued before the dogs really tangled with him. It took all three of us to place him in the sack. Both dogs were so paralyzed from the cramped position that they had to be dug out. They were badly gashed from spikes and Tarzan's teeth, but it was the lack of space which saved the dogs and Tarzan from harming each other fatally.

Tarzan weighs sixteen pounds and coons are famous fighters. Few dogs matched in weight can stand a chance with them. Often a coon can lick three dogs each twice his own weight. Their extremely loose, thick skin is of great use to them in escaping a stranglehold. Nothing seems to daunt them. Coons have been known to face four dogs and two men without a sign of fear and never once losing their amazing presence of mind.

TARZAN, THE RACCOON

But facing a wife is something else, and that night when Tarzan was let into his cage we stood for a long time laughing as we listened to his shrewish wife give him a scolding after almost a week's absence. We didn't hear Tarzan say a word!

Next day we discovered that several of Tarzan's front teeth had been knocked out of line and so he was taken to the vet and had them pulled. It seemed impossible that he would come through these two experiences and remain as trusting and gentle as ever, but all this made not the slightest dent in Tarzan's slow easygoing temperament.

The next fall I took a vacation and it was my last, because on my return I found that Tarzan had turned up missing one day after having no doubt wandered out of the open cage and into the shrubbery unnoticed. However, three days later he had strolled up the drive at feeding time and calmly entered his cage again. That little episode, along with several others that occurred during my absence, put an end to any serious vacation thoughts of mine from then on.

It seemed that Tarzan had at last settled down to domestic life, for two years passed with nothing to mark the slow days of lolling in the sun and warming his belly. This is a favorite habit of coons who, being strictly night animals, are rarely seen by day even by woodsmen, who have spent a lifetime trapping them. In the wild they spend the day sleeping either in their hollow tree dens, sprawled out on a branch, or in a crow's or hawk's nest high in a treetop where no eye can see them.

Then early in the spring Jane began to make life miserable for Tarzan. The poor old fellow knew no peace by day or night. No matter what corner he crept to she would fly across the cage to drive him from it. A barrel on a stand had to be placed in the cage when she drove him from the sleeping den. She nipped and pushed and screamed at him, but never did he turn on her. All this seemed to point to the arrival of a family, but by the end of June we had given up hope and had all but decided to find Tarzan a new mate, when one night the three babies arrived. In her distress Jane mauled two of them to death. It was days before we dared

113

look at the little female that remained. The cage was partitioned off so that Jane could have the privacy that she so much desired, and for seven weeks Tarzan sniffed at the boards that divided his home. His new-found peace was a luxury, though, and he could

prop himself up in a corner once more with no fear of having his fat belly nipped. Tarzan has the shortest of legs and in this favorite position is a most ridiculous sight. He looks exactly like a square fur pillow or muff with four artificial paws sticking out at the corners. When the Little Tarzana was seven weeks old, Jane brought her down for the first time, and soon after, the partition was removed and the family reunited.

I feel sure that Tarzan would never have lifted a fat finger to devour his child, but Jane would never have tolerated his presence in the nursery. From the moment these two, father and daughter, met, it was a case of pure devotion. The little one ignored her mother and spent every waking moment with her father, playing and romping about him. Young as she was, she showed that mischievous strain that was always to be her outstanding quality. Old Tarzan played back but it was some time before he was able to get into the swing of it. Tarzana never knew when to stop and continued her teasing and capering long after her father was tired. And while her mother gave her sharp words and cuffs, her father spoiled her, took all of her naughtiness, and never disciplined her at all. Her final prank each day was to lie in wait for him as he climbed the ladder up to the den box, when down through the small opening in the floor of the box would come her long monkeylike hand to push him on the top of the head, upset his balance, and send him tumbling down to the ground. By this means she prevented his entrance over and over. Her little pointed elf face with its black mask would then peer down to watch for Tarzan's next try.

It was intensely interesting to see Jane, now five years old, change in appearance. She grew to be a really beautiful animal, her coat darkened and motherhood seemed to gentle her face and erase the wildish look it had always had.

Tarzana's antics seemed to weld the family closer together and soon all of them were playing like cubs at twilight, Tarzana leading and going through her mad routine of leaping, racing over shelf, tank, and teetering barrel. Like the dance of the skunks, the coon's prelude to sham battle is a fascinating rhythmical thing that must be seen to be appreciated. They would approach each other gingerly with a wicked gleam in the eye and head down, and with hindquarters high above the humped back they would tread, revolving the tail in a wide circle. The thick fur and loose pelt rolled and rippled, giving a remarkable effect of motion flowing through every part of the body. Their faces showed the most concentrated watchfulness and anticipation as they waited to spring upon each other and wrestle like bears, or to gallop madly with widespread feet from one corner of the cage to the other.

Tarzana's first winter showed us a little of the close, congenial relationship that exists between coon families in the wild. One coon is seldom found alone in a hollow tree. There are more likely to be six of them — mother, father, and four young ones who are welcomed to the home den until the following April, when the arrival of the new family forces the yearlings out on their own. Many captive coon mothers allow the father to stay at home when the babies are tiny. This may be true in the wild also, though I believe that it has not been proved. However, if he leaves at all it is for only a short time and then he probably goes to one of the several hunting lodges which coon families establish in hollow trees or old crow nests.

Up until this time neither Tarzan nor Jane had ever given a demonstration of the much talked-of but little understood food-washing habit. All three now began this practice that is so strong among wild coons that the specific name of Lotor, the Washer, has been given to them. Food-washing is doubtless a habit formed through having to spend so much time feeling about for what they have caught while it is still under the water, and then washing it free of mud or weeds when they are sure that they have caught something worth eating. They probably just aren't happy unless they can get the customary feel of food rinsed in water. Remember, the coon hunts by night and has no way of smelling, seeing, or hearing what lies in the mud beneath the water. He must depend entirely upon his sense of touch as he squats or wades through shallow water along the shore of stream or lake. This sense of touch is located in the coon's sensitive paws. Truly, he sees with his hands and this is often demonstrated by our three coons. When standing in their bathing tank they feel about with their hands on the bottom of the tank, fingering the pebbles or trinkets that lie there, peering

absent-mindedly off into the distance, but never so much as glancing at what they are 'catching.'

Recalling the frog pond, our unwild coons pat and feel about in their tank in search of crawdads, frogs, turtles, fish, and mussels, and now when fed they rush to the tank to soak and sop their biscuits and chicken heads. They do not wash their food because they are so clean, for they have no hesitation about using the dirty water in the puddle under the tank.

Next to the frog pond the coon loves the cornfield in the season when the corn is in the milk stage. Mice are caught in the winter and are a great favorite in the summer also. When none of these are available the coon will eat anything and everything that can be caught or gathered, including such things as acorns and other nuts, wild fruits and berries, apples, buckwheat, and even leaves and grasses. But he starts the winter with a heavy layer of fat and a fine thick coat of fur, and added to this he dens up and sleeps through the coldest periods of the winter, although he wakens and stirs about when a mild spell of weather occurs.

Tarzana's mischief grows no less. She is no longer the gangly yearling but a tall-backed, long-legged creature. Littlejohn is her particular victim. Let him turn his back on the running hose while filling the tank and she will grab it in a flash and soak him every time. When offered food her slender hands shoot up far above her head to snatch it while Tarzan gently puts up his short fat paws.

I don't know of anything in nature so soft and velvety as a young coon's bare paw, and a tiny coon held in the arms will always reach up and pat one's face with the gentlest of touches. Even old Tarzan's foot is unbelievably soft and uncalloused.

I suppose that to persons accustomed to wild, rangy coons Tarzan doesn't much resemble one, but I doubt if you could find a coon with a more kindly eye, a gentler way, and a more lovable personality. Something in his air and manner makes you stop and talk to him in your most sympathetic voice and look long and deeply into his sad, dark eyes that seem to have grown just a shade less clear lately.

14. Baby Birds

NATURE DOES STRANGE THINGS with some of her young-sters, and sometimes the reasons are hard to find. Why should she deck her young robins with a ridiculous little crown of fuzz? What possible use can it be? It is there when the naked little thing breaks forth from the egg and remains sometimes long after the bird is fully feathered. You might wonder also why the baby robin should have to start life with such a huge frog mouth. The truth is that without this two-way stretch of the baby's mouth there would be no room for the parent birds to plunge their own beaks far down the baby's throat in order to place the food at that one spot which causes the baby to swallow. As it grows and learns to pick up food for itself, the large mouth opening is no longer needed and begins to diminish in size.

Strangest of all is the great potbelly that baby birds have. It not only takes care of the enormous amount of food they need but also serves as a third leg, a pillar of support to keep them right side up and to prevent them from losing their balance before their weak feet and legs begin to be used. Without this big heavy belly, they would be blown from the nest or crowd each other out.

Every neighborhood is blessed with some child or grownup to whom everyone comes for help when birds or animals are concerned.

ANIMAL INN

These are the folks who drop everything and gather up their gloves and basket and go out to rescue the run-over pup, the cat on the roof, and the motherless robins and cottontails, and if you are one of these who open your home and heart to every stray and homeless waif, perhaps Trailside's long experience with young and injured creatures will help to solve some of your problems. Of course, it's pretty certain that if you are an old hand in these matters there's not much that you don't know about what to do when the time comes — but for those who are just beginning here are some pointers to tide you over.

Any spring morning you are likely to find a young robin sitting on the front walk. He appears to be lost and may even let you pick him up. But no doubt his two parents are out wearing their beaks down to the nub in an effort to feed him and three others and hoping that, if they leave him alone long enough, he'll use his keen eyes and spot a worm for himself. This is the difficult period in the life of the young birds, robins especially, and it is far better to let the older birds train him as they see fit. They coax him up out of harm's way when roosting time comes and he will learn to eat alone much quicker with their care than with yours, providing of course, that he can fly and isn't a bird that has fallen or was taken or flew away from the nest too early.

If he is one of those little misfits who should be safe at home in his nest and can't fly or eat by himself, then there's not much to do but adopt him. Proof of his babyhood may be found in several ways:

1. His breast should be speckled instead of robin-colored.
2. He should sit squatting on his heels as he would in the nest and refuse to walk or stand up because he is not yet ready to do these things.
3. His downy crown of feathers should still show a little bit — although this is not essential.
4. His tail and wings should be short and stubby although he is almost fully feathered except perhaps for some bluish pinfeathers.

5. His mouth should be big enough for you to be able to stick your finger in it and should have a yellow hinge of skin at the corners.
6. He should sit with his head held rather high and open his mouth hoping for food whenever a hand passes near him.

He'll probably be very tame when you take him in and sit trustingly wherever you put him, because he seems to know that it's up to you or someone to fill his mouth several times an hour.

Sometimes — when you are quite sure who his parents are — it may be best to place him up off the ground in the shade in the hope that they will come down and feed him. If you can find an old robin nest to put him in, so much the better. If not, put him in a strawberry basket lined with dry grass. Of course, he will have to be taken in at night and put where he'll be warm. But get him out again early when his folks are hunting worms. However, because of weather conditions, in most cases you'll have to take him in right from the start and adopt him.

The kind of nest your adopted bird sits in before he is able to stand on his own two feet is very important for the development of those feet. Nature designs nests to serve special purposes. The young crow, hawk, and jay need nests of rough branches and twigs so that their growing feet may grip the branches and exercise their muscles. The baby nighthawk is quite content with no nest at all because he is hatched on the ground. The young owl needs the dark seclusion of a box similar to a hollow tree trunk, while the scatter brain and aggressive sparrows do quite well in the bottom of a very small carton floored with sawdust with straw over them at night for warmth. Robins need the firm, round, cup-shaped nest to push their feet against. A radical change of nursery often produces crippled feet or weak legs — so here is a fine chance for you to try to build a suitable nest. An old robin nest supported in a berry-basket if it won't stand by itself is, of course, the best, but you may have to try a small strainer or bowl or a shallow box lined with hardened mud or clay.

Food, however, is your first problem and since one baby robin

requires about eighteen feet of angleworms a day you'll find that you can easily keep two men and a boy busy digging for them! It's much easier to fall back on a less natural diet that is equally nutritious, and there are a number of foods suitable for baby birds including some of the cod-liver oil preparations sold for hand-fed canaries. Always be sure that the food is fresh, moist, and warm, that is, neither hot nor cold. For nestlings, including the very young babies and those still in the nest but feathered, use:

Boiled mashed potato mixed with hard-boiled egg yolk, half and half.
Raw ground beef or horse meat.
Baby-chick food called Growing Mash mixed with a bit of wheat germ and moistened with water. Mix as needed in a small dish.

122

BABY BIRDS

Older birds just out of the nest and those still dependent on hand-feeding will want the above diet, especially the raw meat, plus:

Raisins soaked overnight in water and drained.

Mashed fruits.

Grated carrots and other vegetables.

Ground rape-seed is rich in vitamin B and may be added to any mixture.

Cod-liver oil supplies A and D vitamins but should be used in very small quantities mixed with the food, as in feeding numbers of birds one teaspoonful only is used with each pound of food mixture.

By the second day you will begin to appreciate what it means to be a mother bird, but think how lucky you are with only one fledgling to take care of! The bird, too, will help you to get that mother-bird feeling because by that time he is sure that your mission in life is to supply all of his wants, and you only need tiptoe near him or whistle to have him pop up like a jack-in-the-box and scream his lungs out for the food that he is sure you are bringing.

Getting the food in his mouth is usually no trick at all when you have mustered courage enough to ram it far down his wide throat. For this purpose you may use the tip of a pen holder, an orange-wood stick, a match, or, better still, an eyebrow tweezer that's not too sharp. He will be no end patient with your first clumsy attempts to aim without hitting his eye, but if you fumble too long he will finally collapse in a heap. Work quickly now and be all ready when he bobs up hopefully again with wide-open mouth. Don't be afraid that he'll choke; baby birds have no instinct to swallow until they feel something touching the back of their throats. When he has had enough he will cease his loud, anxious food calls that are never omitted after he reaches a few days of age.

After each feeding, he will carefully place his droppings outside of the rim of the nest so long as the makeshift nest you have provided is nearly like a robin's nest in size and shape. At this age the black and white droppings are encased in a clear mucous sack which parent birds grasp in their beaks and carry far from the nest, so that the location of the nest is never revealed to enemies by the presence of droppings. You'll never succeed in keeping him or his nest as clean as a mother bird, but do your best. Small squares of cleansing tissue or paper napkins in the nest, changed at every feeding, will help some.

Do not give a baby bird water unless it is panting and exhausted from long exposure in the sun or heat and then give it only a few drops. Baby birds do not know when they have had enough liquid. The food you prepare should be moist enough to take care of its needs. Too much water causes death quickly. He is ready for water when he is old enough to know water when he sees it in a dish. Care must be taken not to wash the worms that he is fed unless they are well drained.

Feed him whenever he cries or opens his mouth. In between feedings he'll catch his forty winks of sleep but he won't mind about when you're not getting your nap. By five o'clock he is usually tired of it all and willing to release his human slave until about seven in the morning. You will find it most difficult to resist the plaintive calls that percolate through your morning dreams and if you don't rush down and mix the baby's formula before you do any other chore, you just haven't the necessary qualifications for a mother bird, and his reproachful voice will tell you so.

But if you love young things, you won't find this a hardship. Those bright little eyes that follow your every move, that insistent voice and fluttering widespread wings somehow compensate for the scores of times you stop to feed and care for him each day. Mother birds brood the young often by sitting close over the nest. Because of this any little bird that is being hand-raised will sit contentedly covered by your warm cupped hands. He will learn to accept your finger as his first perch and can easily be taught to sit there for each feeding. In the wild, flight comes with the development of the instinct of fear and once out of the nest fear prevents the bird from ever returning to it.

And so one day this youngster will stand up on his legs and

make his first flight and more than likely it will be to your hand or shoulder. But he will still want and need to be hand-fed for some days. About this time he will enjoy a bath twice a day in a shallow pan about six inches in diameter. He will also need a cage with a perch or two, but do not use a canary cage, which is designed for a small bird. A robin soon damages his flight feathers when they touch the bars at every turn.

Slowly his mouth will appear to grow smaller and smaller and the yellow hinge will shrink and fade until hardly noticeable — although traces of it will remain through the fall to mark him as this season's brood, as will his speckled breast. Of course, being hand-raised he knows a good thing when he's found it and he will try every means to fool you into supporting him for the rest of his life. Picking up food for himself is the last thing he plans to do, but it is well to begin to place a dish of food along with fine charcoal and bird gravel or black dirt in his cage so that he'll be forced to begin to eat by himself. If he is used to worms put them in the dish and their wriggling may attract him.

When he eats and drinks by himself, it's time to release him. But if he is too tame be sure that you release him where he won't land on an unfriendly shoulder. And then say good-bye to him forever, because birds do not return to the spot where they were raised or first knew the outside world. They only return to the area in which they themselves built a nest and hatched their own young. It would be fun to welcome them back, but there would hardly be room for the birds raised by Trailside were they all to return each spring.

It is harder to raise the naked, scrawny-necked nestling, with his big potbelly that serves to anchor him in the nest. The greatest danger is the chill that he is likely to suffer at night when the temperature drops suddenly. It is always safest to place an eight- or ten-inch square carton over him at night. The nest itself may also be placed in a deeper container to prevent him from tumbling out. Air holes are not necessary; no box is so air-tight that holes are needed. The heat of an electric bulb during the day is just enough to keep him warm. A small red bulb may be used at night. Very tiny young birds do not always peep for food but any sudden sound or a slight touch on the nest will send their slender stalks of necks shooting up to an amazing height. After being fed they instantly fall asleep, so don't be alarmed if your fledglings are discovered

with limp necks hanging over the rim of the nest. If you don't believe that all is well just give the call you use for them or tap the nest. The little yellow heads will bloom like magic!

Some experience is often necessary before you can identify these naked birds as well as those just feathered out. Sparrows are very tiny and twitter constantly but soon begin to hang on to the matchstick or tweezers like bulldogs. Almost immediately they peck the food from the feeding stick. They are at the same time very shy and scuttle to a corner of their box before and after each feeding. Robins have yellow throats, while bluejays have a lovely, fresh rose-pink throat lining. Starlings are tough when they hatch and will skate across a table top on their naked bellies and pin-feathered wings as fast as a lizard. They are dull gray and have low-set eyes. Among the sweetest of baby birds is the rose-breasted grosbeak which looks like a large brownish sparrow with a coarse beak. They are delicate feeders and their call is a plaintive little whistle. The males soon show their pink underlinings to the wings and a faint strawberry stain on the breast.

Baby nighthawks are almost impossible to hand-raise, for

nighthawks are insect-eaters who feed on the wing. The young and injured among insect-eating birds can rarely be coaxed to eat in captivity. Baby nighthawks are owlish looking with mottled gray feathers, almost invisible beaks, huge frog mouths, and short legs. They behave well and stay where they are put, but it is difficult to persuade them to bob at their food. Fortunately, they require far less food than other birds and as their parents feed them only two or three times a night, they will feed best at twilight. They prefer meat and a mixture of egg yolk and mashed potatoes.

Birds that cannot be helped are best chloroformed. To do this place the bird on a cloth in a coffee canister or glass jar slightly larger than the bird. Pour a couple of medicine droppers full of chloroform in the bottom of the container and cover the can. The bird will die in a minute or so.

Holding a bird when you wish to treat or examine its injuries can be very simple for both of you, if you'll spread the first two fingers of your left hand in a V shape. Then with the palm of your hand placed over his back grasp the neck firmly in the fork of the V. Form a 'basket' of your thumb and remaining two fingers and enclose its body. The bird may be carried in this manner for a great distance and there will be no danger of squeezing it or of pulling out its feathers in an effort to hold it from struggling. A great many baby birds are killed by heat exhaustion when a child's hot hand confines it too closely. With your right hand you can flex each leg and wing to see if it springs back in place. Slackness shows a sprain or break. In older birds an injured wing often heals without help, but is never quite so good as new. A young bird with a broken wing is best chloroformed. Thigh breaks in both old and young usually leave the birds hopeless cripples. A very fine job may be done in repairing a leg bone when the break occurs between the first two joints, if the break is clean. If you are clever at these things, you can do a great deal with the gauze tape that sticks only to itself, cardboard splints, or those made of balsa wood. Birds have a marvelous power of fighting off infections so that medications are not necessary when the skin is broken. The main thing to avoid is the tight bandage or adhesive tape that confines the lungs or causes the leg to swell. From May through September something like three hundred young and injured birds, of about thirty different kinds, are brought to the museum by bird lovers. They range from the tiniest kinglets to the big herons. About half of these survive to be released. A few birds that are permanently disabled and unfit for life in the wild become members of the Bird Hospital — a very large cage with plenty of flight room. It houses several different kinds of birds who all live peacefully together and fill the museum with song even in midwinter.

15. Tarbaby and Domino, The Skunks

WE WISHED FOR ONE. Two would have been unexpected luck and so when the call came that there were five tiny baby skunklets that would be ours for the taking, we could hardly wait.

The dew was still glittering on the grass when we arrived at the old monument factory near the vast cemeteries in the suburbs of the city. These areas with their acres of undeveloped land are sanctuary for many small wild creatures. Penned outside in a corner and snug in a dark packing-box were the five toothless or-

129

phans, who two days before had greeted the care-taker in the yard of the plant when he arrived at work.

Five nurslings such as these would have been fast asleep in their mother's den at this hour had she not met with some accident, and so there was nothing for him to do but gather them up, feed them warm milk, and find them a home. The four of us got on our knees and the stone blocking the door of the box was carefully moved aside. We could hear a snuffling and churring inside. Small, pointed, black faces topped by white fur night caps appeared and disappeared at the door. There was much stamping and snorting when a hand reached in to coax them out and then we learned that though the skunklets were toothless, they were not defense-less, as one after another fired its pygmy stench bombs, until the combined barrage of ten small field-pieces kept us dashing from the scene of attack. Finally, and with renewed speed, we gathered them all up and got them to the cage in the car. Then, with windows wide open, we drove the twelve miles back to Trailside in record time, stopping only long enough en route to purchase two bottles of deodorant.

The odor of skunks at close range has been accurately de-scribed as a mixture of cabbage, garlic, onion, sewer gas, and sul-phuric acid. Wafted from a distance on the night air it is enjoyed by most nature-lovers because it has a not unpleasant musk that speaks eloquently of dramatic happenings somewhere deep in woods or meadows. But it is the distance that lends enchantment. Smelled indoors or on one's person, the smallest particle of the fluid has a most unhappy effect upon everyone. Naturally, young skunks have only a small supply of the fluid. It is perhaps due to the quantity rather than the quality that the odor fades rapidly from even the skin or hair. Life becomes quite bearable again only a few hours after one is exposed to it and by the second or third day there is no longer any trace of it.

For the next few days after their arrival the white danger flags on the tips of their tails were seldom at half-mast. The litter was marked in what is known as the short-stripe pattern. A Jiggs-like upstanding cap of white tapered off nearly half-way down the back in two streamers forming a V. Skunks with the longer, wider stripes are more striking and beautiful but since the white part is hair and will not take the dye the furriers value them less because the stripes must be cut from the pelt before they are all dyed a matching black.

Our babies, four males and one female, were at first glance all but identical, but there were three sizes of white nose blazes and four sizes of tail tips, so that if we consulted our chart we could distinguish one from the other providing they would hold still long enough to be examined! By the evening of the first day, however, there was one that could be identified in the dark merely by touch. His personality came up out of the heap with a warm friendliness. When I put my hand in the cage, the new Tarbaby, so named to take the place of one long since lost, would put soft forefeet on my wrist or lay his head in the palm of my hand. The others stomped and bounced backward on their short legs until they danced on their front feet. It was Tarbaby who was always first to come forward to sniff or snuggle. As the days passed, he grew more and more friendly.

And then, too, there was the tiniest, the runt who seldom walked without both ends pointing in the same direction so anxious was he to threaten us with his miniature danger. But after the first night there was never an attack. Threats, yes — alert tails, stamps, aimings, everything but the final volley, and so by the third day we were handling them in the careless manner that veteran drivers of dynamite trucks handle their cargoes. We even tempted them to go so far as to protrude their two white ducts, but they had adopted us as their humans and had joyfully substituted any boy's shirt for their mother's safe den, and bread and milk in a dish for her nourishment. Dry bedded and well fed, with each other to cling to for animal warmth and comfort, I'm sure that they missed their mother very little.

They weighed about six ounces each and were round balls that could be cupped with ease in one hand where they slept like little black cherubs. After looking into so many brown and buff-colored faces among the rodents, these black ones were a startling novelty. Their big heads and wide, toothless pink mouths, their large flat tongues, their shiny, bare, black feet — everything about them was exotic and we could only think of them as funny and adorable little black pickaninnies from the jungle.

But these infant contours and that indescribable air of the nursling fade so swiftly and imperceptibly that you notice no change until one day you realize that you are holding the miniature of an adult skunk and not that roly-poly creature of a few days past, whose four feet gathered together into a bunch up near its large nose when it lay in a milky stupor on its back in your hand.

The sanitary and bedding arrangements of five unweaned skunks was at first a problem. The small cage on the front desk was necessary for easy and constant handling but while their legs were so short, sawdust was not practical because they were covered with it at every tumble. Hay bedding terrified them and they ignored woolen blankets. On cool nights they would sleep in a small carton into which they fitted like licorice drops but we soon ran out of cartons of the right size because if you give a skunk a corner he'll use it for sanitary purposes as soon as he gets through sleeping in it.

TARBABY AND DOMINO, THE SKUNKS

They soon settled down by preference in one end of the cage on smooth newspapers. In the two far corners they carefully placed their droppings and since these are more like those of a cat, the papers at one end of the cage needed changing many times during every hour. This was a troublesome chore but at the same time it was funny to see one sleeping skunk after another waken and crawl out from the heap and waddle to the other end of the cage and carefully use a corner and then crawl back to the sleeping heap. In a week or so as they grew steadier on their feet and increased in height it was more practical to use sawdust in the far corner.

By the sixteenth day their teeth were through the gums, they slept less, and although they continued to have about five feedings of milk a day, they were ready for the bigger and permanent cage. The only cage suitable was that of John, the white rabbit. This was a floor cage with a sliding tray of sheet iron seven inches deep, this feature being essential for skunk caging. The highly indignant John was ousted and the five skunks installed. John never used this cage, which was always open for him to come and go as he pleased, but just the same it had been his for three years and he knew it and to this day he makes every effort to occupy it and shows his displeasure quite often by stamping up and down in front of it.

At this time the skunks began their daily trips to the big outside play cage. Here they played in the sun, wrestled, and trailed each other in single file and found new corners. They also found their first victim when they ganged up on a healthy, young, but too trusting robin who was trying his wings in the sun for the first time. When discovered, the five culprits were busy plucking the feathers from his dead body in the darkness of the den box which they shared with a turtle or two. When the bird was given to them as their first

133

solid meal, a tug of war followed in which the bird disappeared. The next day it was necessary to remove from the cage three young mallards and a visiting duck. The little skunks had turned hunters.

Three weeks after the arrival of the five skunks a farmer came to Trailside with a basket containing four more babies of exactly the same age and size. There was nothing to do but take them in even though we already had three skunks too many. The old Chinese proverb, 'Be careful what you wish for, you are apt to get it,' came to mind. Somehow I had wished a little too hard for a skunk. The new babies were generously marked with white and thickly furred. Two broad bands of white ran from cap to tail and each had a lot of white on the tail in varying patterns.

But there was plenty of room for four more in the skunk cage. The new litter was placed with them and left alone for several hours during my absence. Upon our return to the museum on that warm, sultry night we sensed what had happened as we turned in the drive. The odor grew stronger and stronger and when the door was opened we heard the sound of a baby skunk squealing. It has several times been stated that the skunk is a mute animal. Seton describes their calls including the mating call, which I have never heard, but I have found that young skunks are among the noisier babies, grunting and squealing over food and bed and sometimes seeming to buzz and churr in sheer good spirits when charging one in play. An adult male that I once had would go into a perfect fit of temper at feeding time if not served as soon as he smelled the food. He would race up and down and squeal like a pig caught under a fence.

On this night the squeals were like two pigs caught under a fence. Neither the sound nor the odor ceased for some time. The one small male of the new litter was dancing with rage, his back against the wall, and the other eight were charging him one at a time from the other end of the cage. He never paused in his stamping, squealing, and backing up. In spite of his horrible odor, we couldn't help trying to comfort him for here was a case of hysterics that could end only in exhaustion. His musk ducts had been so exercised and strained that they were swollen and protruded and he had backed into the cage side so many times that he was actually bruised. Wrapped in a thick flannel and petted and talked to he began to calm down and like a tired, frightened puppy, he gradually relaxed and showed signs of grateful relief as he fell asleep. Why he should have become so terrified of the other skunks and his own cage mates, I do not know. I did not get the impression at all that they were picking on him and I believe that their charges were merely efforts to satisfy their curiosity regarding a skunk who would use his defense on one of his own kind, an unheard-of breach of etiquette so far as I am able to learn.

Some time later in the evening we placed him once more with the others but the whole thing began all over again, so that night he slept alone and all of the next day he had sudden fits of combined panic and rage and drove the other eight to the corner. This new litter was quite different in temperament from the original five and for some days each little family clung together, even choosing separate sleeping spots. For two or three days we took turns carrying the new ones in the wide pocket of a carpenter apron to accustom them to handling and we were always just recovering from an attack when another baby would let loose. On the third morning we found the cage at peace and from then on there were no unpleasant experiences, although the new skunks continued to be both shyer and more quick to threaten. Never while we had them did they grow as tame and friendly as the first litter, but this was due in part to three critical weeks of captivity with the farmer who kept them in a box into which he was unable to reach to handle them.

The problem of what to do with seven extra skunks was solved when good homes were finally found for them all. To have kept them several months without their being disarmed would have been disastrous in a public place in spite of the fact that many skunks privately owned can be trusted completely even though they are not disarmed. To have released them after an operation would have deprived them of their only means of defense. And so in two batches they were taken to the veterinary and the delicate operations were performed, the operators being the ones to suffer the greatest, for careful as we tried to be many scent sacks were broken in the process. Due to their small round sizes it took three persons to hold one while the vet made two tiny incisions on each side of the anus in order to reach the white scent gland the size of a large pea, which must be removed along with part of the tube or duct which empties through the anus. No anaesthetic or stitches were necessary as it is a minor and almost bloodless operation. The operation is more hazardous for older animals because the organs are so close to the spine and a false cut results in paralysis.

It is quite possible for a skunk to emit a rather strong odor so long as any tiny part of the gland is not removed. All of ours had perfect operations and healed rapidly with no apparent discomfort at all. When they had been with us for six weeks the six that were left were all having the freedom of the museum. In the morning, during the cage cleaning, they were well able to run for safety when threatened by hasty feet or the indignant white rabbit who still showed resentment when he could manage to get into their cage. They defended the cleaning of their cage with stamps and charges, and only when it was finished would they leave it to pursue the broom and the basket of tools. The mass attack would last five or ten minutes and then each would forget what the original enemy was and begin to charge his companions like small boys showing off.

Tarbaby seemed to do his little dance in a spirit of mischief and teasing and enjoyed being urged on and playfully cuffed or rolled on his back where he would play like a kitten. His charge was a shade more finished. Its rhythm and timing were just that degree more effortless that marked him as an expert. Slap, slap, slap, slap, in rapid succession, were the sounds of his fat-soled, front feet hitting the floor together as he charged in four short bounds. On the last bound he would swing hind quarters and tail high above his back. This dance of the skunks, executed in various directions with an agile twist to the rear end as they aimed unloaded guns, and the frequent change of partners, was most fascinating to watch and listen to.

There was little or no playing in the play cage where they spent the greater part of the day. Here were six big box turtles whose food they could nip away before the slow creatures could finish swallowing it. Here were five ringdoves to chase and remove tail feathers from. There were people to follow up and down along the cage, holes to dig, and a dark box to sleep in such as all skunks dearly love. On hot days the cool sand under it was a delectable bed in which they spent most of the afternoon.

One of their number was given away in exchange for a young crow about the same age. When he came to preside over the play cage he was named Johnnie Crow after the well-known character in the book called *Johnnie Crow's Garden*. The play cage was certainly a real Johnnie Crow's Garden, and was likely to have any sort of visitor that the skunks would tolerate. The skunks and the crow soon took stock of each other and decided upon a mutual respect and tolerance which went far enough to permit their sharing the same food dish. It was as if they felt he was a bird of their feather, for both skunks and crow occasionally teased the light-colored doves.

Toward the end of August, baby coats had been shed and new, sleek coats were almost fully grown out. Of the original nine skunks there remained only Tarbaby and a female whom we named Domino. We could now give them much more individual time and attention. This worked wonders on Tarbaby who, living up to his early promise, began to demand attention. A dozen times during the morning's work I would feel soft pats on my ankles and discover Tarbaby standing at my feet with forepaws reaching up and what passes for a pleading look in his small shortsighted eyes. I would steal a moment and pick him up and he would settle down complacently across my shoulder, content, if it were possible, to cling there while I worked. Meanwhile the jittery Domino with her permanently upstanding tail capered back and forth, hoping for a pat but too slippery to be willingly caught.

These two, almost identical in markings and size, are entirely different in attitude and temperament. Domino enjoys playing but often plays for keeps and her nips seem a little less friendly. She has never completely surrendered to handling, and by that I mean she squirms and clutches with her paws when we try to coax her to relax and lie belly up. Not so Tarbaby who has forgotten long ago, if, indeed, he ever knew, that one's underside is the weak spot and should always be protected against injury.

Busy days find Tarbaby strolling among the museum crowds, never excited, never in a hurry, pausing with drooping, white-plumed tail to be admired and petted and perfectly at ease when lying stretched out on his back in someone's arms. How right was my guess that first night when, having saved the name for years, I called him Tarbaby after that other one who wandered off into the woods so long ago.

16.

Bullfrog

ONE COLD, AUTUMN DAY a boy brought to Trailside a big bullfrog that measured five inches from his nose to the base of the spine. His legs made an additional seven inches. As this bull-frog was lame and didn't leap to escape from the big tank, as so many bullfrogs do, we decided to keep him. He had beautiful yel-low-green eyes like jewels. The black pupil was rimmed with a fine gold line and the coppery iris was flecked with glittering gold dust. We knew he was a male because the circle of skin called the tympanum which is stretched over the inner ear was much larger than his eyes. In females the eye and the tympanum are about equal size.

His tank is eighteen inches wide, thirty inches long, and eight-een inches deep, and is covered with wire mesh. A cave of rocks in the water is his favorite hideout and there he sits on the sandy bottom with just his head out of water. That first winter he had to be forced to eat. Twice a week I wrapped him in a wet cloth to keep a firm grip on his slippery muscular body and pried open his

139

strong jaws with my fingers. When he clamped his mouth shut over one of my fingers, his mouth remained open just enough so that an ounce or so of raw meat, cut in small pieces, could be poked in. Each time that I let him close his mouth to swallow his big pop eyes would drop down and close tightly until they were level with his head. The bullfrog, like all frogs and toads, actually uses his eyes as food pushers because when they drop down into his head they fall into two little pockets in the roof of his mouth and help in some measure to force the food down his gullet. Toads and frogs cannot blink to shut the eye because the upper eyelid cannot drop down over the eye. They do, however, have a third eyelid which flicks upward and covers the eye with a thin, almost transparent membrane.

When we had had him for two years, someone again tried to feed him raw meat dangled from a string to imitate live prey. He snapped, got it, and shoved the string away with the back of his hand. Our feeding troubles were at an end. He even took food from our fingers after that.

In the spring when the marsh marigolds and skunk cabbage were up, we brought in big, wet clumps of them with the heavy clods of soil and moss still massed about the roots. We put them in his tank and admired him as he sat among the green and golden plants in the earth-stained water.

The next morning at dawn loud and terrifying sounds came from the sleeping museum. It was only our big bullfrog celebrating spring as his ancestors did. The voices of those primitive amphibians are thought to have been the first voices heard by the silent, new world made up of the first air-breathing animals, and so theirs was the first of nature's spring songs.

The deep, resonant calls from a bullfrog pond can be heard five miles. Indoors the slow roar does not have the same melodic qualities as it does when heard on a warm spring night out-of-doors. Our bullfrog often calls when there are a great many people talking loudly in the museum. He sounds then as if he were all out-of-sorts and complaining about the noise.

BULLFROG

When his back is gently scratched, he swells up and reminds us of the frog in Aesop's fable who tried to puff up as large as an ox. This puffing up is one of the frog's only means of defense because, when he fills his body with air until it is two or three times its normal size, he isn't so easily swallowed by snakes and other enemies.

When we go on scratching his ribs he continues to keep his head down, his eyes closed and his body puffed and seems to enjoy being scratched because like other animals he leans to whichever side is being scratched.

Each time that he outgrows his skin he sheds the fine top layer of it and although it is usually found in pieces at the bottom of the tank sometimes we find a ghostly white glove, delicate as cobwebs, with all the fingers quite perfect, floating on top of the water. Once in a while we catch him in the act of shedding and the bits of wrinkled skin hang in shreds on his body. Every so often he slowly raises a big webbed hand up to his nose in an effort to dislodge the old skin.

17. The Whitefoots and the Meadow Mice

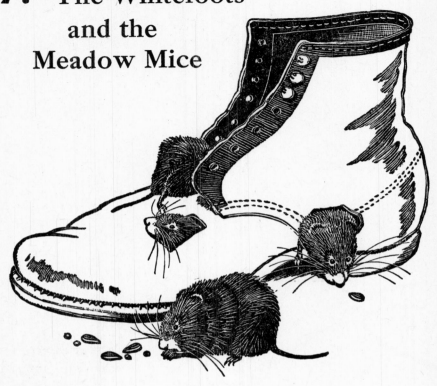

BEFORE ME is a small glass-walled world covered with wire mesh. In the dry grass at the end of the tank is a hollow section of log about six inches in diameter neatly stuffed with shredded corn-husks. It could only be the home of small tidy creatures. Hanging above it in one corner is a pear-shaped hollow gourd with a small opening. Crammed to the very door are sunflower seeds and corn. A gnarled and crooked root twines about through the upper part of the tank and at the other end is a nine-inch exercise wheel. On the floor of this little mouse acre is fine dry sawdust. The label on the tank reads:

THE WHITEFOOTS AND THE MEADOW MICE
WHITEFOOTS ARE THE SQUIRRELS
OF THE MOUSE WORLD

These whitefooted mice climb and leap and like squirrels gather nuts and seeds and store them for winter use. Nests are built in burrows, stumps or often high above the ground in a hollow knot hole. Winter homes are sometimes bird nests which have been roofed over.

There probably isn't another animal in America as exquisite or as beautiful as the whitefoot, and it would be hard to choose the prettiest among their great numbers, for there are more forms of them than any other kind of native animal. This is not to be wondered at, since they are to be found from the high forests of Panama

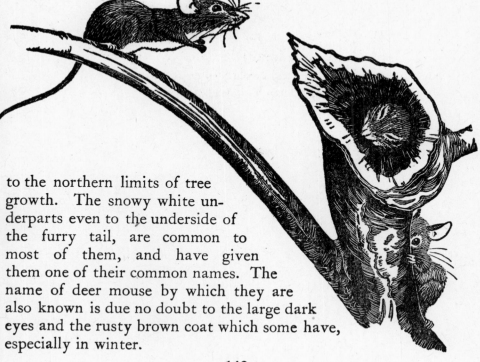

to the northern limits of tree growth. The snowy white underparts even to the underside of the furry tail, are common to most of them, and have given them one of their common names. The name of deer mouse by which they are also known is due no doubt to the large dark eyes and the rusty brown coat which some have, especially in winter.

The Trailside collection includes both the local brown-coated ones, varying in color from light brown to almost black, and several of the lighter creamy breeds which were purchased at a pet store, as well as two albinos. The albinos are not to be confused with the common white mouse used for laboratory experiments and also popular as pets from times unknown. Their odor alone distinguishes them from the whitefoots, which are quite odorless. The laboratory mouse, which is the same species as the house mouse, has an overpowering odor.

Truly these tiny woodland whitefooted mice are the squirrels of the mouse world. Their choice of dens in hollow trees, their ability to construct a nest from grasses and rushes at the top of two cattail stalks, their hoarding of small nuts and seeds, and their agility and grace, are all habits and traits patterned on the same lines as those of their bigger cousins, the tree squirrels. Like squirrels, too, they love to winter indoors, especially in summer cottages near the woods. Spring-cleaning discloses all their little treasures, such as hollowed-out cherry pits and rose hips hidden under pillows and in old shoes. But with the mild weather they go back to the woods, leaving the pantry not nearly so tidy as their own clean storehouses in the treetops. Even their length of life corresponds somewhat to that of squirrels, for these are thought to be the longest lived of any of our native mice. One captive lived almost six years and was doubtless older, since her exact age was not known.

Whitefoots also have a strong homing instinct and experiments have shown that young mice will return from a distance of two miles to the home stump from which they had never previously ventured more than a few yards, and will do it in two days!

Occasionally one of the Trailside mice escapes. If it is not discovered by one of the several animals who roam the museum at night, we usually catch it again by setting a box trap on the floor under the table where the deer-mouse tank stands. The homing instinct brings it back to the location of the den. Late one night I surprised a mouse running in frantic circles under the table where the tank stands. In the dim hall light it was as gray as a house mouse, but I took a chance and caught it in my handkerchief. In the tank and under bright light it proved to be a very soiled and hungry and thirsty whitefoot which had been loose I don't know how long. While he ate and drank a dozen mice gathered around and inspected him from head to toe. Since he was one of our albinos there was no doubt that he was not just a stray mouse.

Casual observation doesn't reveal much of the family life of mice, especially when individuals of a large group are hard to distinguish from each other, but one amusing incident that occurred at Trailside is worth telling. Mice are the very best of mothers and just as savage about defending their young as larger animals are. Of course, there isn't much they can do when danger threatens except to take their babies along and run for their lives. This is not as difficult as it sounds, because eight babies can hang on to the mother's nipples. A mother deer mouse who was living with her mate in a very large cage became frightened and dashed from the nest with all of the babies attached. The father raced after her trying to herd her back. When he failed he tried pulling her, but that wouldn't work either, so he yanked one baby away and carried it to the nest, came back for another one, and only after he had separated her from three of her babies did she cease dashing about and return to the nest. This may prove that mice are also good fathers!

The only little person I can see before me now in the whitefoot tank is fast asleep in a small, hollow branch. He has such a smug look on his face that I can easily imagine the mousey dream dancing in his sleepy head. All day there has been no sign of a living creature, but now that it is dark the activity will begin. There are small rustlings in the hay in the corner and I can just make out that there is much coming and going between the hollow log den and the airier hay nest in back of it. Suddenly four mice come out, two from each end of the log. There is a mad race for the corner and for a while it looks as if every mouse is going to be on the top of the heap. But since that is impossible they settle down at last. The one at the top has quite a time keeping his balance and when washing starts, as it always does when a whitefoot arrives anywhere, the heap is really hard put to keep the arrangement.

Now two mice are inspecting the food store — the hanging pantry that, in their mousey minds, is to tide them over winter's famine weeks when ice glazes every wind-rattled seed. One mouse has the most amazing appearance. His cheek pouches, which open in the inside of the cheek, are so stuffed that his nose is as square as a shovel. Many small creatures such as chipmunks, pocket mice, and kangaroo rats who must make winter stores, have been provided by nature with this means of transporting their harvests to their hidden granaries. Then, inspection done, for some reason important to mice and unknown to men, every one must be in the very same corner at the same time. Suddenly, all of the shoebutton eyes close, the large, nervous ears, thin as silk, fold back, and all are asleep.

Many of the whitefoots have lived in this glass world for several years. Although they do not hibernate in the wild, collecting stores for winter use and hoarding them away in a safe place is the law for whitefoots. When the first breath of autumn is in the air (goodness knows how they are aware of it when they live in a glass tank), the gourd, which is their summer home, begins to get more and more crowded with food saved out from the day's generous rations, until one morning the whole pack of whitefoots, crowded out by their own thrift, are dis-covered asleep in a heap in some corner, while the gourd is filled to overflowing with grains. Then the log 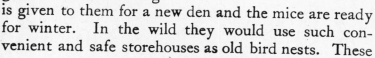 is given to them for a new den and the mice are ready for winter. In the wild they would use such con-venient and safe storehouses as old bird nests. These also serve sometimes as winter quarters for the mice themselves and, cleverly roofed over with twigs and leaves and grass, they are snug and safe hide-outs in the wildest winter weather.

The heap of mice in the corner has awakened now and several more have come out of the log. Although I have never seen white-foots play with each other, they are all evidently having a very gay time. Nobody walks, everybody runs — over the twisted roots and through the log, their long whiskers vibrating rapidly, as they sniff at the top of the tank through which come all the odors of the outside world. One mouse has settled down inside the cup of mixed grains and two are sitting up eating dainty morsels of raw carrots and apples which they hold in their forepaws. Another is digging in the sawdust like a dog for a bone. His front feet are just a blur and the sawdust flies out in a steady spray as he kicks it back with his hind feet. Now he tucks a grain of corn in the hole and covers it and rushes to the top of the tank along the roots, where he leaps to the wire mesh and explores all of it, traveling upside down as easily as a fly would.

One of the youngest, easy to recognize by his large head, has begun his evening practice. For weeks he has been trying to run the wheel which is still too heavy for his tiny strength. Round and round he whips, but the wheel never moves. After every few jumps, he runs to the edge of the wheel and peers over, as if looking for what might be keeping it from moving. He has become quite expert at handsprings both forward and backward and seems never to tire of doing them. He makes haste to leap into the wheel whenever any of the old mice start revolving it and then what fun he must have racing along beside them, but in a short time he is back again at his endless cartwheels. He is determined to work that particular wheel and will have nothing to do with a lighter, smaller one offered to him. All mice, even house mice, love a wheel. A newly captured mouse of any kind will enter a wheel almost as soon as he is placed in a cage. When there is no wheel, many whitefoots find a spot on a branch near the top of the tank where they can turn handsprings by kicking off from the wire mesh cover.

'Ah, what a fine, fat storehouse we have!' seems to be the general opinion in the mouserie. Everyone must scamper up and have a look at it, squeeze inside and mill around in it. A mouse will leap from the food dish to the top of the log and stand on his hind legs just for the sake of peering in at the golden grains and then, as if satisfied that all is well, hurries back to his interrupted meal.

And yet with all of this activity there are never any arguments in the whitefoot tank. A newcomer sometimes must battle for membership for a week or so before being accepted as one of the group. Although some species are known to have a birdlike trill, our mice have never made a sound, even their babies are as 'quiet as mice!'

The activity among the whitefoots has been steadily increasing while I have been watching. Their feet move more quickly than the eye can see and the mouse tank has the appearance of a Christmas village scene in a toy shop in which little mechanical figures run by clockworks are all moving this way and that, in and out of doors at a mad pace. Suddenly, as if the clock stopped, the mouse tank is quiet. It is eleven o'clock. The last mouse has slipped into the log den. The sleepyhead snug in his hole wiggles out backward, yawns, stretches like a cat and daintily scratches an ear with his hind foot. In the midst of his face-washing he stops to sniff the air with twinkling whiskers and tumbles pell-mell down the branch and into the log as if he suddenly remembered an appointment.

The whitefoots are not the only mice to have a tank in our museum. There is a second, in one corner of which a high-topped shoe house painted green with a window and a door cut in the side stands against a heap of hay. The label on this tank reads:

MEADOW OR FIELD MICE ARE THE MUSKRATS OF THE MOUSE WORLD

They look very much like muskrats and are good swimmers.

They are born scrappers. They have to be! Because they aren't the best climbers or runners.

Under the long grasses of the open fields are hundreds of their nests connected by a network of runways through the protecting jungle of grass stems.

All evening there has been no sign of anyone appearing at the door of the shoe house, but from time to time I can hear the sounds of a miniature dogfight. Such quarrels are common in meadow-mice families. These chubby little fellows are naturally scrappy. Even their babies can be heard all over the museum squealing, growling, and quarreling among themselves just as humans do sometimes.

Since it is not at all late for meadow mice who are active both during the day and at night, we shall turn them out of their shoe and see whether they will be as busy as the whitefoots were all evening.

ANIMAL INN

It is somewhat of a shock to many persons, whose ideas of mice are based on the mousetrap variety, to see for the first time the field or meadow mouse, who is as different from house mice or white-foots as a shaggy Shetland pony is different from a sleek, trim race-horse. The long fur of the meadow mouse has the dull color of the ground dweller and burrower, and since they are neither good climbers nor swift runners they have learned to stand their ground and to fight savagely. Their shape and color, their short tails, small eyes, and small ears have a striking resemblance to those of the muskrat, who is truly only a larger and more specialized meadow mouse and closely related to them. Oddly enough, although the muskrat is native only to the new world, the meadow mouse is found all over the northern half of the world. Ponds and streams are attractive to them as home sites and when their burrows are placed in the banks, the mice are sometimes seen diving and swimming even under the ice like miniature muskrats as much at home as in a cornfield or meadow.

But in spite of their pugnacious temperaments the four adult battle-scarred little warriors who have just been awakened are far less nervous and excitable than the whitefoots. Even their whiskers move less often, which seems to indicate that their daytime activities, in contrast to the nocturnal habits of deer mice, have caused the meadow mice to depend less on their sense of smell and the important sense perceptions furnished by whiskers. They are not so gentle but neither are they so timid and shy as deer mice. One is now busy running the wheel and the other three have settled down in their customary pyramid on the flat rock in one corner of the tank. Although two are wideawake one is slowly bending over farther and farther until — can I believe my eyes? — he slowly topples off the rock on his head, gets up in a bewildered way, and then brushes the sawdust from his nose and climbs back up on the rock.

This rock is part of the sanitary arrangements of the meadow mice. Their droppings are never to be found anywhere except in back of the rock in the corner. Their supply of drinking water is suspended from an inverted bottle stopped with a rubber cork through which a bent glass tube runs, because for some curious and unexplained reason, droppings are always carefully placed in ordinary water cups when they are at hand. In the wild, the meadow mice concentrate the droppings at intervals along the runways, usually at the mouth of a burrow, indicating that the den is kept clean.

The mouse in the wheel looks quite different from those on the rock. As he runs his body stretches out long and slim. He has grown tired of running straight ahead in order to turn the wheel and has begun to wind in and out between the spokes. This amazing trick of theirs seems impossible when the wheel is spinning so fast.

The birth of babies in this group of meadow mice is rare enough to be the cause for much excitement at Trailside. The babies are naked and toothless until the fifth or sixth day and the spot of milk shows plainly through the skin of the stomach. Not until the eighth day or so do the ears and eyes develop enough to open up. On the twelfth day they are weaned, and all during that nursing period it always seems remarkable that such tiny creatures will have the instinct to scratch their ears and wash their own faces.

To match the story of the deer-mouse father, there is one told by a careful observer carrying on some breeding experiments in a laboratory colony. A mother meadow mouse had one half-grown daughter as well as a new litter of still naked babies. The temperature of the nest compartment was very low and as there was nothing with which to cover the babies the mother was unwilling to leave them. She solved the problem by dragging in the older child and dumping her in the nest. This had to be done three times, and with nips and cuffs, before the young daughter understood what she was expected to do and stayed obediently to play her part as unwilling nest-warmer until the mother returned from feeding.

When not running the wheel or eating, the meadow mice spend much time sitting contentedly as close together as possible in the wheel or on the rock. They have no winter pantry and in this region never put aside winter stores. In the West, the Plains Indians and the Dakotas gathered a great many of their own winter supplies from the stores of the meadow mouse native to the region. It is rather nice to know that some of the Dakota squaws placed corn or other food in the burrows when they took the valuable beans of the industrious mice who sometimes had stored as many as fourteen quarts of them!

The winter store is not necessary to meadow mice in this region because food is always available. Underground they can find tender shoots, tubers, and dormant sprouts that lie at the heart of the grasses and sedges. Stems and seeds of both are also eaten. Much damage is done to young fruit trees when they gnaw the underground bark and should they circle the tree completely, it is doomed to die before the damage is dis-

covered. On such a diet, meadow mice are able to carry on as usual in spite of deep snow on the prairie and meadow.

Most of their lives, in fact, are spent sheltered from the open sky where hawks and owls cannot find them quite as easily as they would if the meadow mouse didn't build his miles of grassy tunnels. Three or four often come together in a small open space five inches in diameter. Others slope up to the surface of the flattened meadow grass and may be seen dotting the ground at frequent intervals.

These narrow, well-swept avenues are constructed by their gnawing away grass stems at the roots and bending over those along the sides of the path to form a tunnel or arbor. Holes along the way lead down to underground nests but many nests are woven of grass with a side opening and located under rocks or planks or in the base of large tufts of tall grass. Snow must only serve to make these nests and runways snugger, for the meadow mice never winter in houses and barns.

Mice play many interesting parts in the scheme of things. And when Darwin said that the old maids of England had a great influence upon the quality of beef produced there in his day, his reasons illustrate Nature's great law of cause and effect. To begin with, old maids keep cats, or at least they used to! Cats hunt field mice; empty mouse nests are favorite nests for bumble bees; the bumble bee is necessary to fertilize red clover; clover when ploughed under makes for a soil rich in nitrogen; rich soil produces good pasturage and fodder crops, and without these two there can be no fine quality nor quantity of beef produced. Therefore, old maids who keep cats have a great influence upon the quality and quantity of beef produced.

There are many accounts of mouse plagues even in recent years. As they can eat over half their weight in green stuff in twenty-four hours it is not hard to understand how a plague of mice can upset the whole agricultural scheme of the area until the mouse population is cut down by lack of food, by disease, or by an increase in the meat-eating birds and animals who flock to an area overrun by mice. Mice of all kinds, and meadow mice in particular, because of their large numbers and wide distribution, are an important part of the diet of owls, hawks, foxes, raccoons, snakes, skunks, weasels, and other predators. Sometimes there aren't enough mice to go around and during those years of food scarcity there are fewer meat-eaters, but often more destruction of game animals by the predators. No creature, however powerful or predatory, including man, can escape his part as a link in some food chain. All of the food chains upon which life is built have their beginnings back in the vegetable world, the green world. Blood calls for blood, and the endless mouse hunt is carried on without let-up, but those creatures which live upon meat alone hunt the vegetable-eaters, the humble little grass-eaters who bear their young often and in great numbers. These vegetable-eaters are all of the small rodents, and it is the mice of the world, the meadow mice in particular, who feed more hungry mouths than any other species.

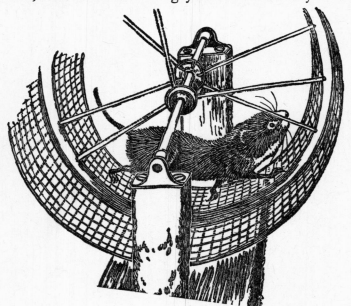

18. Buster Brown, The Red Squirrel

AS I WRITE, there is great rejoicing at Trailside, for Buster Brown has come back! The news is announced as each friend of Trailside comes in the door. We can talk of nothing else and a dozen times a day this tiny whirlwind of a red squirrel is taken from his cage to be petted and played with all over again. His special friends have been called on the telephone and have hurried over to rejoice with us. Buster himself seems the most pleased of all. It has been three months since Buster romped and played with his favorite humans and Trailside hasn't been the same since the awful day in November when I opened his cage and out popped a red demon of ill temper. Buster hasn't really been away — it is just that he has two personalities and for three solid months without a let-up, he has shown us nothing but his very worst one.

The coming of his autumn bad temper corresponds with the coming of his winter coat, which is a change from the sleek brown summer coat to the thicker fluffier one of winter, marked with a glowing chestnut brush stroke from head to tail-tip. This coloring is beautiful and brilliant in contrast to his olive-colored sides and soft gray underparts. Beneath the top fur you catch the several color bands of each hair, as on the hair of the white-tailed deer. Furry ear-tufts are also a part of the weatherproof costume which has the finespun texture of a bird's plumage. But to offset all this finery there is Buster's bad temper.

The bad temper of a red squirrel is one of the small but more terrible things in Nature; though perhaps it only seems so because a red squirrel is such a tiny handful of satiny elegance. He is one of the elfins of the animal world and among the many kinds of squirrels there are none with such winning ways, such speed, grace, and beauty, nor are there any with so great a capacity for sheer merriment.

Added to these charms, Buster's friendliness was always so gay and unreserved, his sense of fun so dependent upon people that if there were a shoulder to zip around and pockets to explore he never dreamed of leaping to the floor or venturing beyond his small corner of the museum. But in a temper his face is distorted with rage as he opens his mouth wide, showing four long teeth, and with his head thrown back sings forth his anger in what resembles a particularly vicious-sounding alarm clock. His emotion is so violent that it jars his front feet into a rapid stamping. Let anyone so much as come near his cage and he bounces around and around and up and down, screaming, buzzing, and chirping. It doesn't matter whether he is at work on a nut, for food never interferes with his anger. He goes right on muttering and shrieking between bites. Perhaps it is the concentration of so much rage in one of such tiny size that is so appalling.

This is the second autumn of Buster's life and I remembered that during the first autumn he had experienced a mild spell of bad temper which passed in a few weeks. This autumn at the first indication of a loss of gentleness I decided that this unhappy mood was to be a yearly affair. So that Buster's friends wouldn't misunderstand and so that strangers would not think that we were

156

keeping captive a miserable little half-tamed beast, I put up the following sign on Buster's cage:

Go away! I hate everybody! — that is, I do at this time of year. Every fall I get a wild streak of bad temper. I guess it's the call of the wild. There's nothing to do but wait until I get tame again. Then I'll be my old self — friendly, playful and gentle.

On his worst days food could be poked through a hole in the cage wire, preventing his lightning leap of attack or escape. Cage-cleaning had to be done by stealth at night. Carefully the jingling keys were fitted in the lock, silently the cage door was opened and in a flash the two den entrances were blocked tight and the light switched on. Like a furious bumble bee, Buster buzzed and tore at the rags which made a prison of his beloved den. It was now righteous anger which shook his fiery little soul, for his deep and inborn sense of personal possession was being outraged. His home, his castle, the only thing he could call his very own, was in danger, and we had to do our work swiftly, because it is not pleasant to strike terror to a small householder.

Once a week during these three long months, Buster was al-

lowed to run free in the museum for a little while. Like a demon on wings he would dash to the basement and into every room of the museum in search of victims. Other caged squirrels were attacked through the wires while never for a moment did Buster cease his cries of challenge and hatred in all keys. Finally, when he was panting for breath, I would put on gloves and sadly collect the biting, scratching squirrel and lock him up for another week.

But as the weeks passed, I began to believe that Buster Brown, as I once knew him, was gone for good. Gone all the gentle little mock-fights he once loved, gone the quick response to his name, and the lightning leap at the snap of a finger. It had seemed almost impossible to me that in the wild the red squirrel makes life so miserable for the fox and gray squirrels that they soon retreat if they by chance wander into the pine forests which are the red squirrels' domain. I could now perfectly understand with what horror the bigger, slower squirrels looked upon an enraged pygmy such as Buster.

I had given up all hope and was making plans for his release in the North woods with the coming of spring, when one day as I opened the cage out popped the old Buzzy Brown, playful, affectionate, and sweet-tempered. With dizzy spirals and agile loops, he zipped over me from head to toe and came to rest on my bare arm. Surely he was only planning to sink his teeth into my skin. But no! He slid into his favorite position sprawled belly down on my raised elbow and rubbed his cheeks along my skin. With some doubt I lowered my arm and said the magic words, 'Want to fight, Buzzy?' Like a flash he was squirming on his back in the crook of my arm pretending to be fighting for his life — his eyes squinted shut and all four feet rapidly cuffing at my fingers. Three months of unabated fury and then this silly mock-fury and kitten-play! No one can tell me that animals haven't a sense of nonsense! Buzzy remembered everything, his name, all of the little eye-baffling tricks, how to tug and gnaw at fingers without hurting. It was amazing. After half an hour of the wildest glee and activity, he let me pick him up and place him back in his cage without protest. These are days that every animal keeper records with pleasure in the daily journal.

So now that Buster is back and his story has a happy ending, I can tell you a little about his way of living and how he came to Trailside. His tameness and trust are all due to the fact that he was a hand-raised baby rescued when the nest, which had been built in a Wisconsin woodshed, was destroyed by accident. Although this is frequently a favorite nesting site, no one dreamed that a mother red squirrel had chosen to build in the woodpile, and so the owner's dog standing near-by, who probably knew all along, managed to destroy all but one of the four blind babies that fell to the ground. This baby was Buster, tiny, weak, and unable to stand on his own legs, for a new-born red squirrel weighs only a few ounces at birth. For weeks, his first human friends fed him from a medicine dropper, washed the milk from his face, kept him warm and tried to make up for the loss of his mother by teaching him how to have fun in their way. They paid no attention to strange sounds which his wise mother would have told him to listen to, and they never thought of teaching him to be afraid, and so like most bottle-fed animal babies, he grew up without any doubt that everyone was his friend.

Only a baby weasel is as elegant as a baby red squirrel. Buster was a tiny, silky brown mite with a wise but astonished expression and the close-set pointy ears and white-rimmed eyes of his kind. This facial expression has stayed with him although he has all but doubled in size. He now measures seven inches from nose-tip to tail-base, and weighs eight ounces.

When he was about ten weeks old he wanted no more milk and began to eat nuts and seeds, raw fruit and vegetables. But a pet squirrel baby in the country was a different problem from a pet squirrel growing up in the city and so when vacation in the North was over, Buster was brought to Trailside. Young as he was, he immediately set up housekeeping in a perfectly orderly fashion. All extra nuts, bread crusts, and bits of fruit and vegetables were stored in the wire basket which hung in the corner of his cage and which took the place of convenient forks in tree branches and old bird nests which red squirrels use as storehouses and drying racks for mushrooms, berries, and other perishable food supplies. No other American squirrels practise this nor do any others collect their winter stores in but one or two hiding-places such as a hollow tree or a stump. Only the red squirrel preserves green pine cones by wedging them between the rocks or roots in icy springs. Other squirrels are content to bury single nuts in the ground where they or their comrades may return to dig them up when needed. Pet fox and gray squirrels litter their cage floors with half-eaten food. Not Buster. Every smidgeon goes to the pantry. Buster, of course, often does bury single nuts under the leaves that floor his cage and if he is busy gnawing when you approach, he will either bury the nut or run up and drop it in his main storehouse, the wire basket, before he comes to the 'poke hole' which is a broken place in the cage wire, to give you his undivided attention.

Buster Brown lives, like a busy red dwarf, in a tin-floored cage, 24 by 32 by 36 inches, with several sturdy branches on which to play and a carpet of leaves or pine or spruce. His den is a hollow tree-stump nailed to a thick square of wood. When he first took up quarters there several days of tedious gnawing were required before he had enlarged the inside of the stump to suit him. He then began to work on an emergency door at the base of the stump. This took a great deal more time and much of the work was done while he lay flat on his back. Every few minutes toward the last, he would stop work and squirm and wiggle at the tiny arch from one side or the other to see if it was large enough. When he could just manage to squeeze through, he plugged the opening with leaves, content with his hidden exit. For bedding he chose a bit of wool sweater which he unraveled and fluffed out. At four in the afternoon, he goes to bed and nothing but the greatest amount of pounding and coaxing can rout him out. We have long since given this up, because he is so sleepy and bewildered that he simply sits and stares when awakened from his nap.

Buster Brown has made more friends for wild life than perhaps

BUSTER BROWN, THE RED SQUIRREL

any of our Trailside Family. He races over total strangers as if they were long-lost friends, explores pockets and plays hide and seek inside their coats and jackets. He kites through a laughing group from shoulder to shoulder, stopping for two seconds for a boisterous mock-fight and lands on the next person with a tiny squeak. He is a complete extrovert and an incurable madcap, still only long enough to relax for the next burst of nervous activity. He washes his face as if he had to catch a train. Even his scratchings are fun to watch because the speed of his leg makes only a delicate blur. To meet Buster Brown you must meet him *on* your person and have him make your acquaintance as the Lilliputs must have explored Gulliver, the giant. It is a treat few people forget.

19. Bambi, The Whitetail Fawn

'NO,' I SAID, in answer to the voice on the phone, 'a deer is a little out of our line. We have no suitable pen and it just isn't possible ... but all right ... bring him over. The children will enjoy seeing him and perhaps we can help you find a home for him.'

I was still hoping to think of a person who could be persuaded to adopt a young deer, when the man bringing him arrived. We all dashed out to his car and when he opened the rear door there was a real Bambi curled up like a little ivory and gold medallion on the floor of the car with his big nursing bottle beside him. Unstartled, he raised his lovely head and gazed at us with big eyes, white-encircled. There was no further doubt in my mind about Bambi's future as I reached in and gathered him up in my arms.

We laid him on a blanket in the dim cubbyhole under the front desk and there he stayed, quiet and trusting, hardly aware of the whispering children who sat hugging their knees in the small space before him. At shoulder height Bambi was a mere sixteen inches. Tail and pinkish ears with just a velvet nap of fur were three inches long. His honey-colored coat, still short and sleek, was snowflaked with 'milk spots' and along each side of the spine they were arranged like two perfect little necklaces of evenly strung beads. The milk spots are not lost until the fourth month when the fawns are weaned and no longer in need of the protective coloration which blends so well with the dappled light and shade in the secluded spot where the mother hides them. In this shelter they stay unmoving while danger stalks within a few feet of them for much of the first month of their lives.

Seven weeks before, an Army lieutenant in northern Michigan had found him unwashed and still damp from his birth, trying to suckle his dead mother beside a busy highway. Surely this birth had been before time, for the doe, after being struck down by a passing car, had given life to her three-pound fawn with the last of her failing strength far from the chosen seclusion of the woods. It is just possible that had he not been found another doe might have adopted him, as they often do when a fawn is orphaned.

It was days before Bambi was out of danger and only the devotion of his rescuer and the Army veterinarians had brought him through several severe illnesses. Then, just as he was growing healthy and frisky, the lieutenant received his shipping orders and had only time to drop Bambi off with his brother, who appealed to Trailside when he found a seven-weeks-old fawn somewhat of a problem in a small apartment.

An hour or so after Bambi arrived, he rose to explore his new surroundings. While we all followed on tiptoe and with hushed voices, Bambi began his tour of Trailside, little onyx hooves clicking sharply at each step. At the cage of twittering baby birds he stopped, raised his head slowly on its long curved neck and gazed up at them. A boy's voice fitted words to Bambi's attitude by saying, 'Birds? Birds? Birds?' just as the Bambi in Disney's picture spoke them when he learned to talk. John, the white rabbit, came hopping over and Bambi swung his head to the floor and blew through his soft nostrils, then on fragile legs continued his stroll, with John hopping about him in circles. When he paused, John waited; when he wandered on, John began to hop.

ANIMAL INN

Bottle-time came and Bambi, with white tail wigwagging, disposed of the milk in a few minutes and, butting at the bottle when the last drop vanished, baaed like a young lamb or goat. It was exciting to hear his voice and everyone waited eagerly for that tiny fairy-trumpet sound after each feeding.

The first Sunday after he came, we prepared a Walt Disney setting in the big outside play cage by decking it with the leafy tree prunings that the children collected on the street. Bambi, surrounded by two skunks, several doves, and six young cottontails, was a pleasant surprise to visitors who had not seen him before. We noticed that the young rabbits seemed to sense that there was nothing to fear from Bambi and lay on their sides in the sun without moving as he carefully stepped over them, for, although the skunks never bothered them, they would scuttle away at their approach.

By the fourth day Bambi proved to be a born museum pet, ready and eager for all attentions. His chosen spot was the thick door-mat in the front vestibule and there he rested during the day with his back against the low stone step. Half the fun of having Bambi was to watch the people step into the museum and discover him three feet from the door. Their shock of surprise and uncontainable delight at his unexpected presence there was always a pleasure to witness. Few of the thousands who saw Bambi had ever seen a fawn at all, and then only from a distance and none had ever found one as a house pet.

He accepted devotion and affection as if it were his due and never showed the slightest uneasiness at being completely surrounded by excited children and grown-ups. Quickly he learned his new name and many times a day he would answer to it by rising, by turning in his tracks, or by turning his head and pointing his large ears toward the voice. Dozens of children took turns holding his little cube of salt so that he could lick it and never was a king attended by so many eager hands.

One night after closing time Bambi chased the red setter dog to the door. His mood was unmistakably playful, so we ran and he

164

chased us with white tail high. When the children leaped like goats he leaped, too. He would draw his tiny hoofs up under him and kick out and buck and toss his head. We had many five o'clock romps with him after that, and when the mopping equipment came rattling out of the cupboard Bambi went slightly crazy. It was a signal for a wild race back and forth from front door to back door. As he grew older we had to line up out of the way of his flying hooves and wait until, winded, he would stop and breathe with open mouth. During the hot September weeks Bambi delighted the children by licking their arms and faces and sucking at their hair with his toothless nibbles, toothless because deer have no upper teeth in front. Later many a finger was smartly bitten when its owner could not resist letting Bambi try his sharp molars on them, for his back teeth were well able to grind up acorns and root vegetables.

Bambi's settling down on the door mat was a tricky operation watched and marveled at by everyone. The front legs collapsed at the knee and turned under, then the long hind legs curved inward

close under and toward the front of his body until the front of the hooves rested on the floor. When his whole body was almost on the floor he would uncurve his hind legs and stretch them out or keep them close against his body as a dog does.

One afternoon we took Bambi to the field north of Trailside. He was tiny and so gentle and followed us all so willingly — then Littlejohn came running across the field at top speed. Bambi tossed his head and ran to meet him. The next thing we knew we were in the center of a mad whirlwind. Bambi was racing in an ever-widening circle, taking long spry hops like a jack rabbit, clearing bushes and tall weed patches like a winged creature. The speed of a fawn seems unbelievable. They are well able to keep pace with the mother as soon as they begin to follow her. A whitetail doe can travel thirty miles an hour for three or four miles. The prong-buck antelope is the only American ruminant that can outrun the whitetail. When Bambi at last slacked up, he cantered toward the street and, staying just ahead of his pursuers, began to follow a passing cyclist. Littlejohn caught him a block away in the woods, and then only because he turned back when he saw a dog. That was Bambi's last airing for some weeks.

The public soon learned that two of Bambi's five daily feedings took place at twelve and four, and a crowd would gather to watch the fun. About ten minutes to the hour Bambi would rise and begin to cock long, sensitive ears ceilingward. A few minutes before the bottle was due he would be waiting at the foot of the stairs. On the hour he had ascended three steps still watching and listening. Should there be a delay Bambi would wait only a minute or two and then bound up the perilous curved stairway to wait at the door of the apartment. If the door were ajar, he pushed it open and went straight to the kitchen and standing on his hind legs, he would beat upon the back of anyone heating the milk for his bottle. Those sharp hooves were not at all gentle!

The first few days when Bambi was so tiny and fragile and we feared that he might be accidentally injured, a 'deer warden' was appointed several times a day. This was some trusted child whose

business it was to follow and shield him, and incidentally to run for the sponge or dust pan, because Bambi, unlike one deer I know of, never co-operated in making his sanitary problems indoors less difficult.

In the beginning Bambi spent many evenings in the apartment curled up in a favorite corner near the setter, who mistrusted him completely. Bambi seemed to have no fear of enemies. When the dog lunged and snarled at him, he simply waited a minute before he came back to sniff or gaze at the dog again.

The loveliest recollections I have of Bambi are the times when he stood gazing out of the low living-room window in the evening sunlight. In this light not a hair was lost in shadow and the contour of his pear-shaped head was softened by the long fringe of lashes, the clusters over the eyelids, and the silvery chin whiskers usually invisible in ordinary daylight.

About the time that Bambi was to begin to eat solid food, he came one day and stood beside me as I knelt to feed the noisy young jays and robins who crowded to the door of their cage at the approach of the forceps and bowl of moistened chick mash. Suddenly Bambi's long tongue licked out and snatched the food intended for wide pink or yellow bird mouths. From then on he was not to be left out. As soon as I rose to feed the fledglings, Bambi was clicking at my heels and took his turn with much impatience. We often placed young robins and doves or squirrels on his back and laughed to see him walk about as if this were the most natural thing in the world, and who knows but what it is? Perhaps stranger things than this happen in those secret clearings in the woods where young birds and animals play in the sun.

Toward the last of September his lovely snowflake coat faded and began to come out in patches, giving place to the bluish slate-colored winter coat. He had greatly increased in height and weight, but until he was quite big I would pick him up and hold him on my lap with all of his four legs sticking out straight so that his snowy belly could be stroked and admired by his young friends. Bambi would submit meekly with half-shut eyes. Although he accepted the children's offerings of chopped vegetables and fruits, grain, leaves, and acorns, he refused to give up his bottle. If household clocks were sometimes slow, the little alarm clock in his stomach always knew the correct time for the bottle, and it was far simpler to humor him than to try to break him of the habit.

After a meal Bambi would lie down on the floor beside my chair and await the arrival of his cud, as with many interested onlookers, the cud-chewing business took place. After his delicate sort of hiccup, a hand placed on his long throat would feel the muscles send the cud traveling swiftly upward until it arrived in his mouth. After he had carefully chewed and swallowed it, Bambi and his friends would await the next cud, with such exclamations from the young naturalists as: 'There it comes!' . . . 'See it!' . . . or 'He's got it!'

As with most wild-animal habits and manners of doing things, cud-chewing too has its interesting reason and serves its valuable purpose in being the most efficient and convenient way for this type of animal to procure food. Wild cud-chewers waste no time dallying in the open over food-getting; weeds, the leaves of trees, and acorns are quickly nipped off and swallowed. Then when the largest section of the stomach is well filled the deer seeks the shelter of some hidden nook in the woods safe from the sight of enemies and there he ruminates. To ruminate means to chew again what has been slightly chewed and swallowed before. In order to do this the food collected in the first section of the stomach must first pass into the second section to be moistened. And from there in the form of cuds it passes up into the mouth again. After it is chewed it is reswallowed and this time it is filtered through the third section and into the fourth and last, where digestion takes place.

Bambi's browsing-trees were branches gathered from where the tree-pruners had been at work. His shady nook was a narrow little spot beside a bookcase away from hurrying feet. But when he chose it for his ruminations he was choosing the best possible place that a museum had to offer an orphaned fawn whose instincts directed him like a guardian angel.

I never saw him spit out haw-apple seeds, but after he had chewed a cud made from a meal of them, their clean seeds would be found lying about him in a circle.

When cooler weather came on, Bambi chose a night sleeping-place in a corner free from drafts and with two avenues of retreat formed by passageways between specimen tables. Here he retired at five each afternoon, but later in the evening he was up and about in the company of John, the rabbit, his inseparable companion. When I came downstairs to the museum for a final check-up, I would find the quaintest company of creatures gathered in the big rooms lit dimly by the stair light. There would be Bambi strolling with John, and near-by the two skunks, also Chuckles, the wood-chuck, and often Vickie, the white cat. It always reminded me of the tales in which the toys come to life and talk and walk about at night. For here was a quiet tableau as amazing as any museum could present: six animals each bent upon its own night adventures and explorations, not truly friendly with each other but seemingly drawn to each other's company in no spirit other than a vague sense of sociability. I always got the queer impression that my arrival had caused them all to stop talking.

BAMBI, THE WHITETAIL FAWN

For a long time we had been searching eagerly for the first little swellings on Bambi's head that would mean the budding of antlers. About this time they appeared, or perhaps they had been there for some time, because when we finally discovered them they were up between his ears and not where we had expected them at all. It is the various kinds of male deer which grow antlers (the only female deer having them are the reindeer or caribou), while other ruminants such as goats, sheep, cattle, and antelope, grow horns. Antlers and horns are similar in use but have interesting differences in growth and material. Horns such as cows have are hollow, unbranched, with a strong bony support underneath the horny outer covering. They are never shed and, although they are never sensitive, their growth continues all through the life of the animal. The prongbuck antelope is the exception among American ruminants because, although he possesses horns, they are shed each year.

Deer antlers, which begin their growth in the spring, are of solid bone and are covered with a velvety skin which dries up and peels off after the antler has grown to its full height in late summer. During all this time of growth they are soft and sensitive and, if bruised, grow deformed with extra knobs and points. The antler growth is finished when a tight ring of bone at the base cuts off the blood supply, kills the nerves and causes the bone to dry strong and hard.

The antler is the buck's badge of entry into the great fall tournaments, his shield and weapon when, as a prince of the forest, he battles former companions as rivals for the slim does, who stand with half-grown fawns in the near-by coverts. Three does are thought to be all that the whitetail claims if he is valiant enough to win them. Along with the does go the one or two fawns of the spring before to make up the new family group. By December the victories are all won and the deer made up of these family groups are reunited in a great herd to battle winter, the greatest foe of all. Before spring the wonderful crown of antlers drops off but hardly a month passes before the new antlers begin

171

to grow. Nature allows the proud wearer but four months when the antlers are in condition for use. In April the groups break up, does are seeking shelters for the birth of new babies, and yearling bucks are on their own. Yearling does go off alone too, but later rejoin the mother for another year. The older bucks go their ways in twos or threes, bachelors and good friends until the following fall when they again become bitter rivals.

It seemed hard to believe that Bambi, only twenty-four inches tall with his two tiny bumps, would ever reach two hundred pounds in weight and wear a rack of polished antlers. This first fall he would grow only the little buttons. By next summer he would have two short spikes. The following spring would come the beam bearing one branch making a Y-shaped antler. And in the fourth summer each beam would have two branches or points. Ordinarily a pair of points is added each year but there are many deer that skip or double and, as injuries also cause strange growths, it is not always easy to tell the age of a buck by counting the points of the antlers.

By mid-November Bambi was a problem. Little children aroused the imp in him. At the sound of their voices he would toss his head and prance, so that we were constantly on guard to prevent his injuring someone with his sharp hooves.

Late one Sunday afternoon when the crowds were so thick in Trailside that it was difficult to keep track of him, we decided to end the strain by shutting him in the basement for the remaining hour. I think I had not been back on the museum floor for a minute, when a man came running in from outside to tell me that Bambi was busy shattering a basement window. I arrived downstairs in time to look through the broken window and see Bambi trotting toward the woods. Littlejohn and I followed at once at a fast walk but as casually as we could, calling and pleading. One hundred yards from the museum Bambi paused at the edge of the woods. He had never been free outdoors since that first wild chase; he was snorting from the excitement of his leaps to reach the high table under the basement window and was cut on the hind leg from the shattered glass. Repeating his name over and over, we both ventured at the same time to pet him gently, until I had him in my arms. Bambi at this time weighed no less than forty-five pounds, and lately I had found his awkward weight impossible to carry with any ease. Needless to say I carried him back to the museum with no thought of anything but to get him indoors and prevent his escape to the hundreds of acres of woods and highways about the museum.

This was the beginning of the end. That night I made arrangements for Bambi's new home on a Texas ranch and the next few days were busy ones as we built a huge, solid crate, free of cracks, so that he would have no way of catching his hoof points on them. To make his long journey as comfortable as possible we placed two windows of small-mesh wire in it, floored it deep with hay, carefully fastened in the food and water cans just under the small feeding door, and packed sacks of food to be tied on the outside of the crate for use on the way. Labels covered the crate telling the expressmen just what to do in any emergency.

Express service was in a state of confusion because of priorities of war shipments, and so we tried to prepare for any delay en route. Several days passed after the crate de luxe was finished before the express company could find time and men enough to call for Bambi, and he had ample time to grow accustomed to his box. He ate and slept in it and grew quite at home, even when the door was shut for a half-hour or so as a test to see how he would take to being confined.

The day before Thanksgiving Bambi left for Texas. At the last moment we slipped in his well-worn salt block and snapped the padlock. Bambi's big ears and wide eyes were framed in the little window of the crate as the truck drove away.

He had been a priceless experience for anyone who ever saw him and we knew that many a child would grow up with the memory of Bambi's soft muzzle on his cheek, and that the picture of those large eyes would come before him years from now. We knew that for many there would be no bullet with the name of any of Bambi's kinfolk on it.

ANIMAL INN

For more than a week after Bambi's going John, the rabbit, missed him. By day we should never have known that John felt any loss, but each morning the empty place where Bambi had been accustomed to lie was surrounded by unmistakable signs that John had made many visits to it, hoping that his companion of so many nights would be there to greet him.

Several years have passed, and Bambi's antlers must have a number of points now, but he is still safe on a deer reservation in Texas.

13-1084